PRICING IN A CRISIS PLAYBOOK

A Practical B2B Guide for Pricing with Confidence in a Crisis or Recession

JOANNE M. SMITH

Author of *The Price Negotiation Playbook*

Bradley Publishing

Bradley Publishing

122 Hartefeld Drive,

Avondale, Pennsylvania 19311

First Edition. Printed in the United States.

ISBN 978-0-9897238-3-1

Library of Congress Control Number: 2020906203

Editor: Jeanne Marie Blystone

Cover and Book Design: Karen Saunders & Associates

Contents

Contents

Play 1:
Pricing in a Crisis – The Value of Proactive Planning

Every now and again, our world is turned upside down. We are inundated with news reports that go something like, "We are operating in unprecedented times amidst extreme uncertainty…" Yet historically, every five to ten years something shakes our world — a recession, a pandemic, a significant drop in oil prices and its derivatives, or in some parts of the world — wars, currency swings, or political upheavals. While they may each be unprecedented and bring extreme uncertainty, there is a pattern or commonality to them from which we can learn.

By taking these lessons and incorporating them with pricing best practices, you can strengthen your strategies and plans for existing or future crises in business-to-business markets.

Most crises affect our business's prices, volume, or both, thus creating a disastrous effect on our profits and cash flow. Panic sets in and many businesses and salespeople begin to operate from a reactive mode, often making decisions that unintentionally further depress profits. During these times, it's imperative to proactively and thoughtfully manage the crisis.

If you knew a hurricane was predicted to come through your town, would you prepare? Of course, you would. You'd likely google "Hurricane Preparedness Planning" and get a wealth of information to guide you. Financially related crises should be no different. You need a ***Pricing Crisis Preparedness Plan*** (along with other plans such as supply chain preparedness plans). In fact, a Pricing Crisis Preparedness Plan is likely one of the top priorities, if not the very top priority, you should address.

Pricing, especially in downturns, is essential for the following reasons:

- Pricing is the biggest lever in most businesses for both creating or destroying profits. It is typically a three to five times more powerful lever in affecting profits than volume changes.

- Your customer base, who is also likely experiencing lower demand and declining profits, is likely to step up their price pressure on their suppliers to provide price relief.

- Your competitors, who are also experiencing lower demand and declining profits, may get more aggressive with their prices to ensure they retain their customers, or worse, to grow share.

- Your management, who is taking extra heat from shareholders or senior leaders, may be pushing you to grow volume (good luck in a declining market) or to lower inventory and shorten payment terms to preserve cash flow (again, good luck in a declining market). Both actions unintentionally put pressure on you to drop price.

- Your own sales colleagues, who are worried about their own salary compensation as well as maintaining good relationships with their customers, may begin arguing in favor of discounting to help their customers.

That's a lot of pricing pressure coming from all sides. I can guarantee that if you don't have a Pricing Crisis Preparedness Plan (or the equivalent), you will succumb to this price pressure and you will further destroy your profits. It may be unintentional — a salesperson discounts here, a manager sets a discount there, another salesperson responds to a competitor price discount by matching that discount, or marketing offers a promotional discount price to move off-quality or slow-moving inventory. Before you know it, you've taught your customers that pressuring you for lower price works, and they begin to apply more price pressure. You've also shaken the confidence of your competitors. They now assume you are consistently dropping price, perhaps to target their shrinking volume. And the price war begins. The original crisis that hit you (the one you had no control over), just got infinitely bigger by your actions — the ones you do have control over.

These are tough and scary times, but there is hope. With good planning and discipline, you can minimize the negative effects of the crisis. During the 2009 recession, I was leading DuPont's global corporate pricing organization. At that time, DuPont was a $30 Billion revenue company. Of our over 50 different global business units, the majority were facing market declines of 20% – 40%. The internal pressure on profits and cash flow was immense. To complicate things further, we had just come off a nearly five-year period where we had raised prices quite successfully, yet many of those increases had been linked to our rising supplier costs. These suppliers were now dropping their prices and customers were demanding we push through these discounts. The external pressure was tremendous.

Our corporate pricing group immediately began working with our businesses and providing 'pricing in a recession' planning guidance. We carefully balanced fairness to our customers with fairness to our company. We employed a variety of strategies and tactics from delaying discounts, minimizing discounts, selective increases in certain pockets, to higher discounts in some businesses. The net result was an average decline in our pricing for two quarters and an average increase in our pricing for two quarters for a net $200 million uplift in profits over 2008. While $200 million in profits sounds impressive, both our pre- and post-recession profit uplift from pricing was nearly five times better than during the recession. Had we not taken proactive measures, we would have repeated our history — large price and profit losses in tough markets.

Pricing Crisis Preparedness Plan

A strong pricing preparedness plan has five steps as shown in Figure 1:

1. **Monitoring, Predicting, & Analyzing:** Determining the market dynamics and your historical pricing performance.

2. **Setting Strategy & Tactics:** Setting the appropriate plans to minimize the decline of price and profits.

3. **Building Your Communication Plan:** Developing strong internal and external communication plans to influence behaviors and establish trust with your customers.

4. **Creating a Tighter Disciplined Deal Approval Process:** Modifying your deal pricing and policy approval process to ensure discipline in this chaotic time.

5. **Forming a Crisis Team and Process:** Creating a pricing crisis management team. Implementing and managing the needed processes for success.

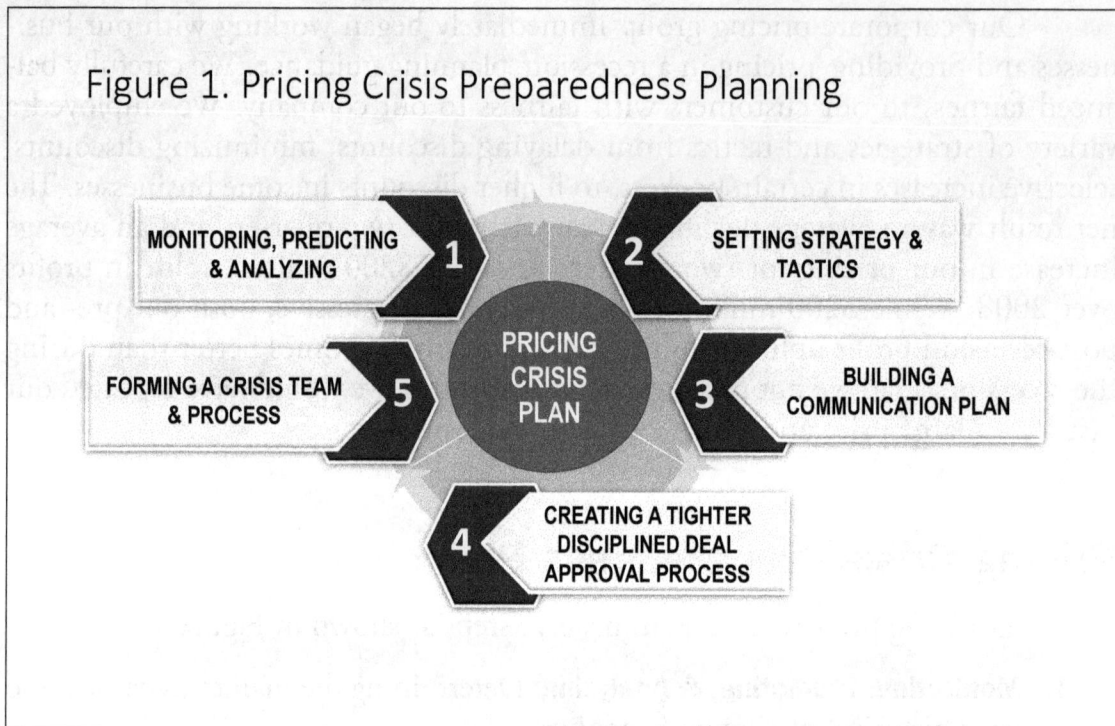

Figure 1. Pricing Crisis Preparedness Planning

This Pricing Crisis Preparedness Plan predominantly focuses on strategy and price setting — often the domain of marketing, product line, or pricing leaders. It delves into price execution especially in Step 3. Pricing success — in good times or tough times – relies 50% on smart strategy and 50% on good execution. Thus, in addition to a strong preparedness plan, your sales force needs to have strong price negotiation confidence and skills.

Price Negotiation Confidence and Skills

Many B2B businesses have highly experienced sales teams that have attended sales negotiation training courses over their career. Yet, the surprising and rather sobering fact is that very few salespeople believe they have sufficient price negotiation skills even under normal market conditions.

I've surveyed thousands of salespeople across hundreds of businesses and found that 95% self-rated their price negotiation skills as mediocre to weak (e.g., on a scale of 1- 5 with 5 being outstanding, 95% rated themselves as 3, 2 or 1). A 5 was defined as "Confident you...

- Negotiate your best price with each deal.

- Get fair price for your value.

- Know your pricing power and use it.

- Increase price with high acceptance success.

- Consistently behave in ways that help market price.

No doubt, these same sales reps feel woefully unprepared for the price pressure they face in a crisis. This must be addressed.

Pricing in a Crisis versus Pricing in Normal Times

The good news is that the principles and best practice behaviors that guide pricing strategy and price negotiations hold in good times and in bad times. However, there are a few additional strategies and tactics that are needed in a crisis including a higher level of discipline. One of the greatest challenges will be maintaining the confidence of the business leaders through the sales team to consistently execute the crisis plan. Pricing is scary enough during normal times and it is even scarier in a crisis. It will test your confidence, your courage, and your conviction.

In addition to concrete strategies backed by solid business experience, case studies will be cited to help you not only build your pricing skills but also to build your confidence in implementing your own pricing plans.

The Structure of this Playbook

This playbook will focus on the five step Pricing Crisis Preparedness Plan and will also provide a condensed study guide on price negotiation skills. For the reader who has a reasonably solid understanding of pricing best practices under normal times, this book will offer actionable, practical advice for implementing foundational pricing strategy best practices during a crisis. For those with less pricing expertise, you will also gain great value, yet you might benefit from referencing my book "The Price Negotiation Playbook" for more in depth explanations.

The End Game

The goal of this book is to help you proactively plan through a pricing crisis and to execute with courage, confidence, and conviction while avoiding the reactive, unnecessary decline of price and profits that typically occur in crises times.

Play 2:
Monitoring, Predicting, and Analyzing

The first step of preparing a pricing crisis plan is to monitor and assess the current market dynamics, predict the market dynamics for the expected duration of the crisis including your projected costs, and analyze historical pricing performance. This is done as a basis for pricing strategy. Analyze this information with an eye for identifying any data or dynamics that justify taking action to increase price, hold price, or delay a drop in price.

Monitoring and Predicting the Market

During a crisis, it is difficult to predict the impact and the length of the downturn. Nevertheless, you will need to make some assumptions — assumptions that you will revisit throughout the crisis. Consider three scenarios: best case, expected case, and worst case. This three-pronged approach will help you develop stronger strategies and contingency plans in the next step. You should focus on the key market aspects highlighted in Figure 2.

Key predictions will include the length of the crisis, the impact on the total market demand as well as on your own demand, the impact on your costs as well as your competitors' costs, and the changes in imports/exports. If data is available from past crisis periods such as the 2009 recession, examine what occurred in your industry as just another input into your assessment.

You'll notice that I've asked you to evaluate both your situation and the industry situation. Generally, any strategy you adopt will have a higher likelihood of success if your rationale applies not only to you but to your competitors as well. In other words, if your competitors are experiencing the same pain as you are, they are more apt to naturally follow — or be influenced towards — a similar strategy. That is a very good thing when your strategy is aimed at stopping price decline.

Perform your analyses at a granular level — by region, by market, by product family, or by product. These may not be impacted in the same way, and if they aren't, then your strategies will likely differ at this granular level.

Consider your competitors and whether they are better or worse positioned to manage through this crisis. Are any of them vulnerable such that they may not make it out the other side? Perhaps their cost base is too high or maybe their technology is too niche or outdated? If so, this might offer you strategy options which will capitalize on their weaknesses. Also, evaluate whether you believe they are more likely to be disciplined or disruptive with their price. Will they be thoughtful and slow to drop price (hopefully) or will they begin discounting quickly and reactively in the false hope of gaining share?

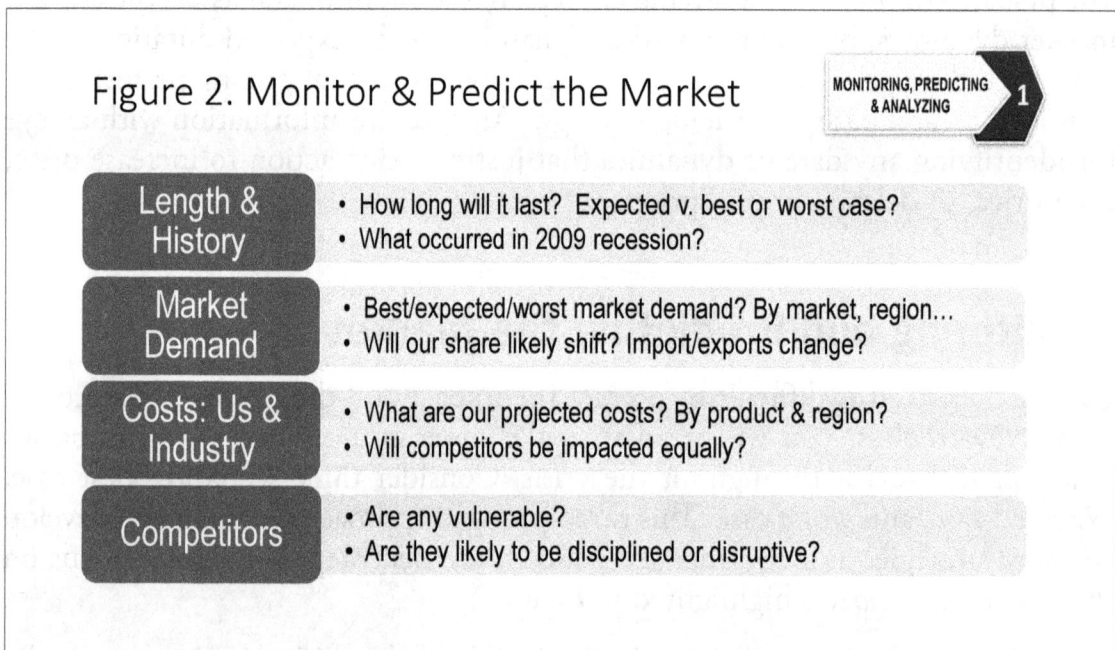

Figure 2. Monitor & Predict the Market

MONITORING, PREDICTING & ANALYZING 1

Length & History	• How long will it last? Expected v. best or worst case? • What occurred in 2009 recession?
Market Demand	• Best/expected/worst market demand? By market, region… • Will our share likely shift? Import/exports change?
Costs: Us & Industry	• What are our projected costs? By product & region? • Will competitors be impacted equally?
Competitors	• Are any vulnerable? • Are they likely to be disciplined or disruptive?

Analyze your Price Performance

Analyze your past pricing and margin performance with an eye towards identifying any rationale that might justify holding price or delaying price discounts. As above, be sure to analyze at a granular level. Ultimately, you will take these analyses down to a customer level.

The approach and success of your recent past price increases will have a large impact on both how your customers respond during the crisis and how you determine your strategy. For example, the weaker your past increase approach and success, the more rationale you will have to hold onto your price. Thus, you have fair rationale and talking points for holding your price if you…

- have not had at least annual price increases, or if you did, but most large/ medium customers never accepted the increases,

- were slow to pass along your own rising costs, or

- had declining margins.

If past increases were done predominantly due to your own rising costs, then customers will demand you pass along any reductions your suppliers might provide to you. Ironically, the customers who will push the hardest for this price relief are often your largest customers — the ones that never accepted or only partially accepted your price increases in the past! They hope you have short-term memories and never go back to analyze just how much price increase they had. Don't provide more price relief than the increases they previously accepted.

Look back at the length of time it took you to pass along increases due to your rising costs. If your own costs increased in the past, yet you took several months to pass along these costs to your customer base, you have a fair rationale for delaying any discounts for at least as many months.

Go back three to five years as you assess your contribution margin trends (gross margin and especially variable contribution margin). Review your revenue, your costs and your margin percent. If you've had a margin percent decline in this period, you have a rationale to hold or delay price drops.

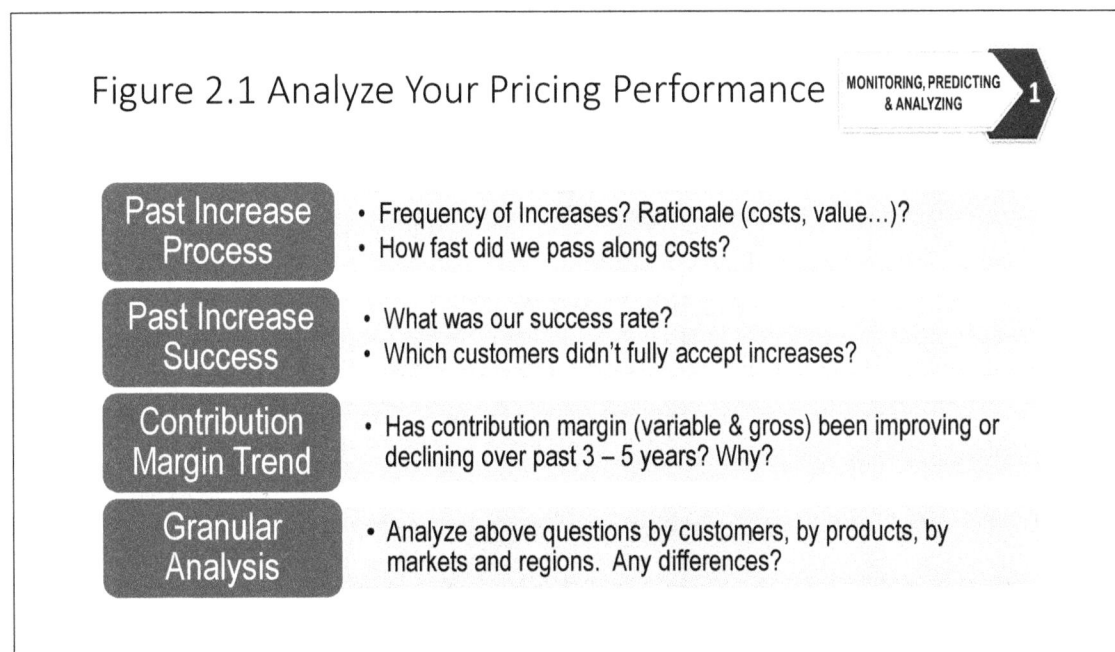

Figure 2.1 Analyze Your Pricing Performance   MONITORING, PREDICTING & ANALYZING 1

Past Increase Process	• Frequency of Increases? Rationale (costs, value...)? • How fast did we pass along costs?
Past Increase Success	• What was our success rate? • Which customers didn't fully accept increases?
Contribution Margin Trend	• Has contribution margin (variable & gross) been improving or declining over past 3 – 5 years? Why?
Granular Analysis	• Analyze above questions by customers, by products, by markets and regions. Any differences?

Analyzing your performance can be done in many ways, yet I strongly advise you to use graphical views as are illustrated in Figure 2.2. Graphical views not only make it easier to see patterns that lead to better strategies, but they are also powerful tools in building the understanding, support, and alignment of leaders through sales — support you will absolutely need. Typical graphs you should consider, at a granular level or at least color-coded by segment, include:

- Customer and product scatter plots: Price or margin (Y-axis) by volume (X-axis)

- Customer price change scatter plots: Change in volume percent over the past one to three years versus the change in price percent (or margin percent) over the same time frame

- Three to five year trend lines: Price, costs, and margin

- Waterfall charts: For key segments and for your largest customers

- Box plots: Price or margin by segment or product differentiation (undifferentiated, slightly differentiated, unique)

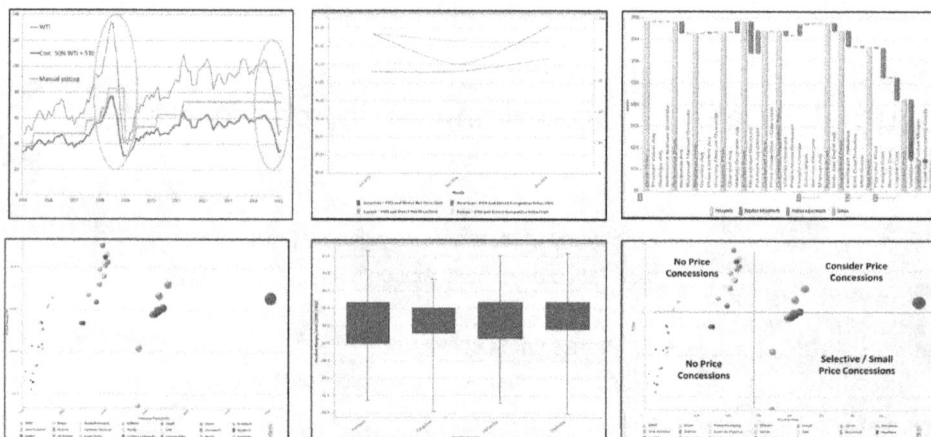

Figure 2.2 Analyze by Region, Market, Product

Play 3:
Setting Strategy and Tactics

Begin by identifying and aligning on any reasonable rationale you or your industry might have for holding or delaying price drops. You might even have select pockets where you can raise price as illustrated in Figure 3.

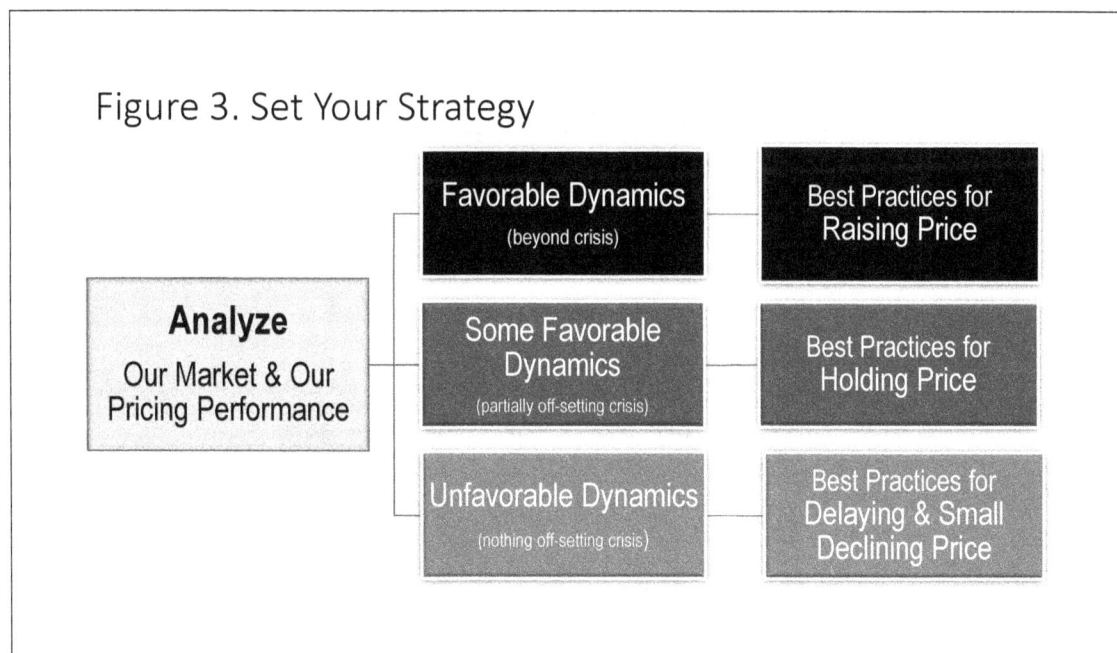

Figure 3. Set Your Strategy

Analyze Our Market & Our Pricing Performance	Favorable Dynamics (beyond crisis)	Best Practices for Raising Price
	Some Favorable Dynamics (partially off-setting crisis)	Best Practices for Holding Price
	Unfavorable Dynamics (nothing off-setting crisis)	Best Practices for Delaying & Small Declining Price

Favorable Dynamics

Favorable dynamics, in good or bad times, which will likely allow you to increase price or at the least hold price, include those listed in Figure 3.1 and especially the few listed below:

- tight supply/demand

- shared pain or rising costs

- competitors increasing price

- market discontinuities that favor your offering

- unique high value offerings

This is especially true if any of your markets are growing or are not negatively impacted by the crisis. You may only need one of the above dynamics to be favorable to trump the downside of the crisis thus providing pricing power.

A word of caution: Market discontinuities might include things such as selling bottled water or hotel rooms into hurricane ravished areas. The demand is suddenly high and people with little choice are willing (almost forced) to pay higher prices. Yet, avoid gouging. Taking excessive advantage of companies or people in a crisis will come back to bite you in the long-term. It will hurt your customer relationships and trust. However, modest increases are worth considering. The odds are high that you will have to add additional costs to supply this demand (e.g., overtime labor, unusual and higher logistic costs, possibly sourcing with higher priced ingredients to quickly step up your manufacturing). You should cover your extra costs adding a small mark-up.

Figure 3.1. Favorable Pricing Dynamics

Favorable Pricing Levers
❑ High capacity utilization
❑ Shared pain/rising costs
❑ Low/lack of price increases
❑ Competitor increases
❑ Market discontinuities
❑ Brand / value differentiation
❑ Growing market / Favorable macro-economics
❑ High entry barriers / switching costs

In addition to the favorable dynamics listed above, dynamics for holding price in a crisis also include:

- The crisis is of very short duration.

- Competitors aren't likely to drop (perhaps because they have a higher cost-base).

- Some customers didn't accept past increases.

  Yet, in a crisis, it is more probable that pricing levers aren't favorable.

Unfavorable Dynamics

Referring to Figure 3.2, unfavorable dynamics which would suggest discounting price, include:

- Competitors have already broadly dropped price.

- You and competitors have experienced declining costs.

- Total market size will be much larger with lower price.

- If you don't drop, the total market demand will drop significantly lower as customers switch to not-in-kind, lower-priced options (e.g., switch from a polymer to wood).

Figure 3.2. Pricing Dynamics in a Crisis

Favorable Dynamics: Hold	Unfavorable: Discount?
❏ You & competitors have favorable dynamics (Figure 3.1)	❏ Competitors broadly dropping
❏ Crisis will be very short-term	❏ You (& competitors) costs are dropping
❏ High value (unique & necessary)	❏ Lower prices will result in total market demand rising
❏ Some customers didn't take past increases	❏ High likelihood of not in-kind substitution
❏ Competitors not dropping	

Again, do your assessment at a granular level. Every product, market, or customer where you can preserve your price will be essential to offset the profit decline from volume or price drops elsewhere.

Fairness and Trust

The rationale for your price moves, in good times and even in bad times, should be governed by *fairness and trust*. Over the long-haul, your prices, volume, and profits will be the highest when the marketplace (e.g., customers, downstream customers, partners, influencers, and even competitors) view you as fair and trustworthy. This is your litmus test. Will your rationale for your pricing action appear fair and reasonable to the market and your customers? They don't have to like your price, but they should feel that it is fair.

Unfortunately, I often see salespeople and occasionally business leaders who appear to forget that fairness applies to both their customers and their company. It is equitable and imperative that you protect the health of your business. It is not your role to bail out struggling customers at the expense of your company's margins. Consider these two situations.

Case Study: *My client, a large provider into the construction industry, was reluctant to increase price and often discounted excessively. Their reasoning was that their customer base (largely small business owners / installers) were struggling to stay afloat. These customers claimed they could not raise their prices to their customers (homeowners or construction firms). My client's behavior was not fair to themselves. Further, they were hindering their customer-base from standing on their own and having the courage to increase their own prices — something they had fair rationale to do.*

Ironically, my client's business was almost underwater for the past five years. If they had not been part of a larger profitable corporation, they would have struggled to stay in business. In fact, the corporation was quickly losing tolerance for this underperforming business; they made significant leadership changes. Many people were laid-off. I was brought in to train over 30 sales teams on effective price negotiation skills. They are now on the road to recovery.

Case Study: *While I was leading corporate pricing for DuPont, one of our businesses announced their annual price increase at year-end 2008, effective January 1, 2009. By late 2008, DuPont was already* *experiencing the effects of the recession which would hit us much harder throughout 2009. It was clear that things were going south quickly. Oil prices were falling, thus we expected price relief on many of our raw materials. Months earlier, I had provided guidance to our businesses to implement any planned price increases in the first half of 2008, given the inevitable market downturn that was coming. This business did not heed that advice — they waited until year-end. By the time their increase was to go into effect, their total market demand was significantly down, their ingredient costs had dropped, and customers were rightfully demanding price relief. Competitors did not follow them with an increase. After all, there really was no fair, appropriate rationale for one. It quickly became apparent to this business that they would lose significant share if they continued to pursue this increase. They rescinded the increase. While this stemmed the volume loss, the attempt at an unfair increase undermined their trust with their customers.*

Raising price when there is no clear and fair rationale, especially when your customer-base would perceive it as distinctly unfair, is not a good practice. Your success will be limited at best and you may hurt your customer relationships over the long-term.

Timing and Magnitude

If you determine that price discounts are appropriate, then every month that you can reasonably delay the drop is crucial. Once again, identify any fair and reasonable rationale for delaying your drop. These might include:

- In past increases based on our rising costs, we took X months before passing them along, thus we will take X months to implement discounts.

- Our margins have been declining for years, we need to begin recovery towards a healthy margin before we can consider discounts.

Just as carefully, consider the magnitude of your discounts and give back as little as is reasonable. For example, if you raised price 10% over the past three years under the rationale of your rising raw material costs and these costs are now significantly dropping, your customers' view of fairness is for you to drop 10%. But consider discounting a lesser amount under a rationale such as the following:

- Our past increases were not solely due to our rising raw material. They also include value-based and competitive-based increases.

- While our raw material costs are declining, our previous price increases were due to far more than rising raw material costs. There were other inflationary costs in our labor, maintenance expenses, and health benefits as well as freight cost increases that are not declining.

- Our past increases did not include passing along our full cost increases. We absorbed a portion of these rising costs.

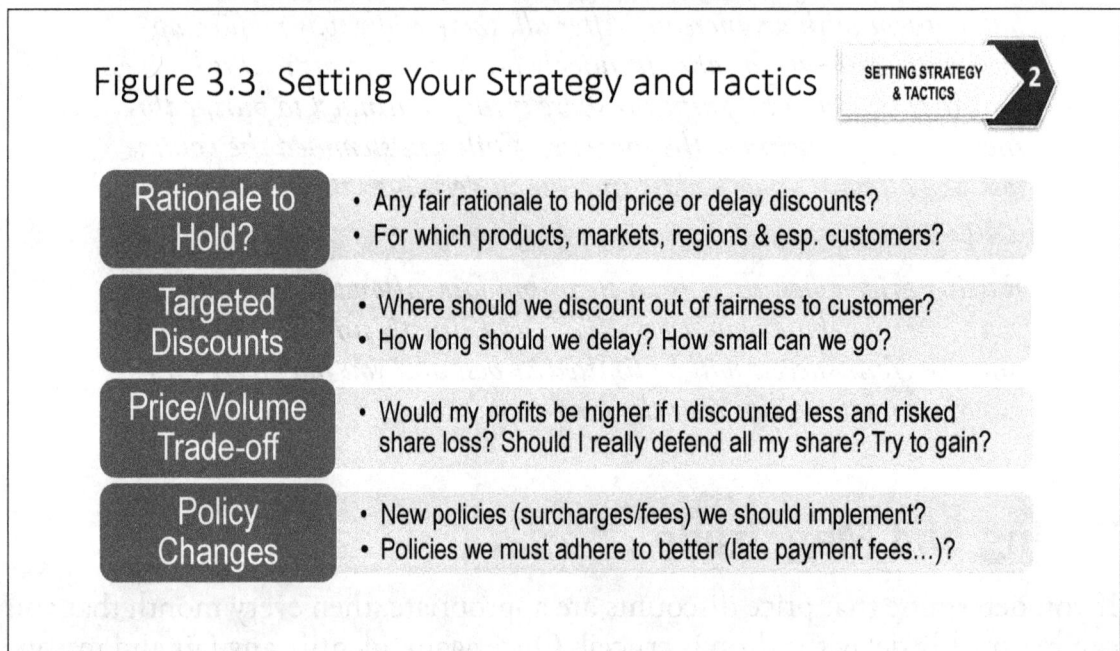

Figure 3.3. Setting Your Strategy and Tactics

| SETTING STRATEGY & TACTICS | 2 |

Rationale to Hold?	• Any fair rationale to hold price or delay discounts? • For which products, markets, regions & esp. customers?
Targeted Discounts	• Where should we discount out of fairness to customer? • How long should we delay? How small can we go?
Price/Volume Trade-off	• Would my profits be higher if I discounted less and risked share loss? Should I really defend all my share? Try to gain?
Policy Changes	• New policies (surcharges/fees) we should implement? • Policies we must adhere to better (late payment fees...)?

Price/Volume Trade-Off Decisions

Once you've determined your strategy and rationale for increasing, holding, delaying discounts, or dropping price, you're not quite done until you consider price/volume trade-offs. These trade-offs are critical yet often overlooked or incorrectly considered elements.

The essential question that price/volume trade-off analyses will answer is, *"Would we be more profitable with higher price and less share?"* In other words, should you increase more, drop price less, or delay drops longer and take the risk of losing some of your volume?

For some businesses, the answer is a surprising "Yes!" However, for most businesses, the answer is largely "No," though they likely have small pockets of products or markets where the answer should be "Yes." Be sure to carve out these unique pockets for a different approach.

The smaller your variable contribution margin percentage, the more likely it is that risking volume for higher price is your more profitable strategy. Thus, if your offering is a commodity or only slightly differentiated, or you're a distributor, then odds are high that your contribution margin is less than 30% – 40% and price is much more powerful than volume in generating profits.

You should calculate the price/volume trade-off for each of your market or product segments, even extending this analysis down to your lowest margin products or customers. The price/volume trade-off calculation for a reactive situation (e.g., a situation where you believe you will lose share if you do not drop price) is as follows:

Reactive Break-even Change in Volume % = Change in Price % / Contribution Margin %.

During a downturned market, if you believe you must drop price 5% to avoid potential share loss, the break-even represents the percent of share you could afford to lose before it would make economic sense to drop your price. For example, let's assume your contribution margin is 30% (the typical Fortune 1000 margin). Also, assume you believe a 5% price drop is needed or you are likely to lose 25% of your market share. Thus…

Break-even Volume = 5% Price Drop/ 30% Contribution Margin or 17% share change

Given the break-even volume is 17% and you believe you would lose 25% (much more than 17%) you should proceed to drop your price.

Let's now assume you believe a 10% price drop is needed to avoid a 25% share loss. In this case, the break-even volume is 33% — far higher than the expected 25% share loss. You should **<u>not</u>** drop your price 10%; it would further destroy your profits.

Rather than calculate the price/volume trade-off, you can use the table shown in Figure 3.3 to look up your break-even volume.

Figure 3.4. Reactive Price/Volume Trade-Offs

Reactive Break-Even Volume for Price Change				
BREAK-EVEN VOLUME FOR PRICE CHANGE	**Reactive Break-Even Volume Look Up Table** Maximum Volume You Could Lose Before Matching Competitive Price Is Justified			
	Price Decrease In Response To Competitive Price			
Variable Contribution Margin	**-2%**	**-5%**	**-10%**	**-20%**
10%	20%	50%	100%	200%
15%	13%	33%	67%	133%
20%	10%	25%	50%	100%
25%	8%	20%	40%	80%
30%	7%	17%	33%	67%
35%	6%	14%	29%	57%
40%	5%	13%	25%	50%
45%	4%	11%	22%	44%
50%	4%	10%	20%	40%
55%	4%	9%	18%	36%
60%	3%	8%	17%	33%
65%	3%	8%	15%	31%

A word of caution. The price/volume trade-off calculation and table listed above are for reactive situations only. Proactive price/volume trade-off decisions are calculated differently. During normal or good market times, you are probably making proactive price decisions frequently, such as "Should I raise price even if it risks volume? Should I drop price to gain share?"

During crises, you will rarely face proactive price/volume trade-off decisions. This is largely because you rarely have the conditions needed to raise price, and crisis times are very risky times to adopt a "gain share though price discounts" strategy. It will backfire on you. You will start a price war and competitors will defend their share. It's a lose-lose situation. Yet, on rare occasions, you might consider a proactive move when you have strong favorable dynamics as discussed earlier, or as described in the case study below.

Case Study: *During a market downturn, a few competitors had far lower costs than several other competitors. These high-cost competitors were vulnerable. The largest low-cost competitor dropped their price below the cost of the high-cost competitors, yet still above their own costs. They targeted the customers of these high-cost competitors with their low prices. After nearly a year and a half, the few high-cost competitors exited the market. This tightened the market allowing the remaining competitors to raise price, thus benefiting them for years to come.*

The case above illustrates how profits are hurt in the short-term (over 1.5 years) yet improves them far into the future. Most management teams don't have the stomach for these short-term profit drops, and even if they do, these high-cost competitors might elect to mothball their operations until the price recovers, later restarting, thus defeating your success. It's not an easy strategy to successfully execute.

If proactive price decisions make sense for you, as they will when you begin to recover from the crisis, then use this calculation or the table shown in Figure 3.4.

Proactive Break-Even Volume (%) = - (Change in Price %)/ (Contribution Margin % + Change in Price %)

Figure 3.5. Proactive Price/Volume Trade-Off's

Proactive Break-Even Volume For Price Change Look Up Table								
BREAK-EVEN VOLUME FOR VOLUME CHANGE	Break-Even Volume Volume You Can Afford To Lose And Hold Profits Price Increase Action				Break-Even Volume Volume You Must Gain To Hold Profit Price Decrease Action			
Variable Margin	2%	5%	10%	20%	-2%	-5%	-10%	-20%
10%	17%	33%	50%	67%	25%	100%		
15%	12%	25%	40%	57%	15%	50%	200%	
20%	9%	20%	33%	50%	11%	33%	100%	
25%	7%	17%	29%	44%	9%	25%	67%	400%
30%	6%	14%	25%	40%	7%	20%	50%	200%
35%	5%	13%	22%	36%	6%	17%	40%	133%
40%	5%	11%	20%	33%	5%	14%	33%	100%
45%	4%	10%	18%	31%	5%	13%	29%	80%
50%	4%	9%	17%	29%	4%	11%	25%	67%
55%	4%	8%	15%	27%	4%	10%	22%	57%
60%	3%	8%	14%	25%	3%	9%	20%	50%
65%	3%	7%	13%	24%	3%	8%	18%	44%

Possible Price Drop Actions

The following are a series of possible strategies or actions you might consider for your business if you are planning on price drops.

Partial-Drop Strategies:

- Consider a partial drop if you eliminated or reduced your typical annual increase in response to the crisis. Credit yourself that amount. Tell customers, "We have already provided price relief by holding off on our annual increase."

- If your past increases were related to your increasing material costs, don't give it all back. For example, if you had increased price 10% over the past due to a combination of cost increases and value pricing, then consider only dropping price 3%–5% when your costs drop.

- Consider only a partial drop if declining material costs are projected to rise again in the next three to nine months.

Delayed Price-Drop Strategies:

- Delay the price decrease for at least as long as you took to raise your price during past favorable conditions.

- Delay the decrease to compensate for margin erosion or very low industry profitability over the past few years.

Selective and Granular Decrease Strategies:

- Only decrease on products materially affected by this unfavorable condition. Hold or increase for products that may still have favorable dynamics.

- Don't decrease equally across all products if they are not all affected equally.

- Focus your discounts on the products that get the most attention from customers (e.g., the big volume products). Don't reduce or reduce to a lesser extent the products that are slow-movers or those which few customers buy.

- Set the specific decrease customer-by-customer contingent upon their historical acceptance of price increases and where their current price is today versus similar-sized accounts.

Temporary-Decrease Strategies: If projections or expectations indicate the unfavorable condition might be of short duration, three to nine months, then consider the following:

- Provide 90-day price relief on select products. If the unfavorable condition continues, you can opt to extend the price relief another 90 days.

- Have the price automatically revert to your current price unless you formally extend it.

Lower-Value Options at Lower-Price Strategies: Good, better, best options can be especially effective during crisis times.

- Develop formal good, better, best offerings through a combination of products, service, and customer experience (F2F sales versus online, only online ordering, etc.)

- Develop customer-customized options: Remove services, no F2F sales, etc.

- Caution: If you are using payment term length as one of your option differentiators, dropping price to get short payment terms is often not a good decision. Price is much more impactful to financial health than payment terms. However, it can still be a good concession if you are forced to drop price anyway.

Cumulative Volume Rebate Strategies: Selectively tie your discounts to share or volume gains.

- Offer price breaks only on all new incremental volume. In other words, your base volume (or share) remains at its current price. Any additional share they shift to you will be priced at an X% discount. This can be done via rebates or a direct price drop for every unit sold over Y units.

- Caution: Large volume gains will result in a negative competitive reaction so be very selective about this move. Further, consider tying the share gain to a longer-term contract — one with price openers.

Industry Policy Change Strategies: Your best move may be to change your policies, potentially leading the industry to adopt more favorable policies. For example, think of 2008 when American Airlines first instituted a fee for checked baggage. Within weeks, most major airlines followed with similar policies. Evaluate the following:

- Lower your price but at the same time institute a desired new policy (e.g., freight excluded, fee for small orders)

- Shift to practices that lower your effort and cost — online ordering, inside sales, inside technical support only, Monday – Friday business hours versus 24/7…

- Shift your value chain model. Perhaps go more direct than through distribution…or just the opposite. Changes of this nature should be carefully considered with an eye to the best long-term solution.

- Enforce policies (e.g., cancellation fees, late fees).

Eliminate Small / Low Volume Product Strategies: This might be an ideal time for some product consolidations to reduce your operation's cost of complexity. Consider the following:

- Raise price on small or reasonably small low-margin products with the goal to either consolidate them (e.g., have customers switch to another one of your products) or to get their margins quite high thus justifying keeping them in your product portfolio.

- Caution: If the product had just been introduced in the last year and has not had time to penetrate the market, consider excluding it from this approach. On the other hand, if this is one of the 'new' products that you keep hoping will take off but hasn't after a few years, keep it in the approach.

- Caution: If your business typically or even frequently runs at high capacity during normal times, then you must also consider the price per time on your assets when determining which of your products are worth consolidating. Products that run very fast through assets help extend your capacity, allowing you to sell more, while products that run slowly through your assets may greatly restrict your capacity and sales during normal times. Under these conditions, it is not uncommon for the most attractive, profitable products during normal times to be among your least attractive, profitable products during crisis times. Keep the long-term picture in mind. Additionally, if during normal times your capacity restriction is due to something such as "insufficient raw materials," then you need to measure and compare your product margin on $ per "restricted raw material units."

Figures 3.5 and 3.6 summarize these potential strategies and actions.

Figure 3.5. Possible Pricing Actions in a Crisis (1 of 2)

Partial Drop	Selective & Granular
• If you didn't yet implement your annual increase, credit yourself (in lieu of...) • If raws are dropping, don't give 100% back if total costs aren't dropping • Adjust if ingredients/oil prices projected up	• Only products materially effected with ingredient price drops • Only top SKU's, fast movers, common • By customer based on past price increase acceptance & margin

Delayed Drop	Temporary Decrease
• Delay decrease at least as long as you took to raise price in past if cost related • Delay the increase to compensate for margin erosion over past few years	• Provide 60 day price relief on select products • Price automatically reverts to current price unless you extend it

Figure 3.6. Possible Pricing Actions in a Crisis (2of 2)

Lower Value Option at Lower Price	Change Industry Practice
• Offer gold, bronze, silver value options at lower appropriately lower price • Remove services, F2F sales, etc. • Caution: Price drop for short payment terms is often not a good decision	• Lower price but institute desired new policy (e.g., freight excluded, fee for small orders) • Shift to practices that lower your effort – online ordering, inside sales... • Shift ratio of distribution versus direct sales • Enforce policies (late fees, expedited fees...)

Cumulative Volume Incentives	Eliminate Small / Low Profit SKU's
• Offer price breaks only on all new volume • Caution: Large volume gains will result in competitive reaction	• Raise price on small SKU's or low profit SKU's with aim of product consolidation • If normal business times are near sold-out, view profit from $/time on asset, too

Policy Changes and Adherence

To offset price declines, consider changes you can make in your policies or in adherence to current policies. You can no longer afford the profit leakage that typically occurs through lack of strong policies or the waiving of existing policies.

Review your policies to be sure you are considering additional fees or surcharges for:

- Cancellation fees or restocking fees

- Small order fees or less than truckload fees

- Late payment penalties

- Credit card payment fees

- Unearned payment term discounts

- Long payment terms

- Extra services (quality control, analysis, special packaging…)

- Expedited shipments

- Long distance shipments (e.g., extra 2% for shipments to California and Canada)

If these policies already exist, be sure you are not waiving these fees.

Influencing the Market

There is one additional step you need to consider before your strategy is complete. You must assess the likelihood of influencing the market — as discussed below and which is probably much higher than you suspect — then set a plan in place. You raise the probability of successfully influencing the market — in good times and in bad times — when you are viewed as "fair and trustworthy" consistently! Figure 3.7 illustrates the best practice behavioral guidelines.

To be viewed as fair and trustworthy, there are three proactive guidelines that must guide your behavior. These are:

- Clearly communicate your intentions.

- Predictably and consistently walk-the-talk (e.g., do what you said you will do).

- Be a disciplined value pricer.

Clearly communicating your intentions is critical to influencing the market. If no one knows your intentions, it's highly unlikely they will follow you. In fact, the more customers and competitors become confused or uncertain about your pricing intentions, the more likely they are to become price aggressive. Customers will not trust you if they don't understand your intentions. Further, effective communications create a sense of fair play across all customers. Customers want to believe you treat them as well as other customers, so they aren't disadvantaged in their market space. Written communications go a long way to fostering this trust. Play 4 guides your communication strategies.

Predictably walking-the-talk is a hard behavior to live up to. It's easy to say you're going to hold price or delay discounts for three months, but it's another thing for sales to hold to this intention as customers aggressively push for price relief. Yet holding firm to your word creates trust. Folding to price pressure and giving discounts (beyond your stated intentions) creates distrust. The customer receiving the extra discount, while happy, is left wondering if they had pushed even further, would you have discounted more? Or, are you giving other customers even deeper discounts because they more effectively negotiate price? These behaviors will train them to always push you hard on price and to never trust the fairness of your price.

Likewise, competitors who might have been inclined to hold price or delay discounts, now lose their confidence and conviction in their own strategy as they hear about you backing off your word. They begin to believe that you are consistently discounting (even if they only heard about one or two situations), and they reactively begin to drop price broadly. The price war begins.

Being a disciplined value pricer essentially means that you understand your value relative to your competition and either price higher if you have a value advantage or you provide a lower-value offering if the customer insists on a lower price. From a crisis pricing situation consider the following basic guidance.

- Even if you must discount, be sure to get a premium over competition if your value is higher.

- When dropping price, use this opportunity for a give-and-take with the customer. In other words, you get something of value for your discounting or you take away something of value to the customer. Customers don't get to have their cake and eat it too. They don't get all your value at the lowest price.

- Especially for your lower-priced customers, be sure to consistently adhere to your policies related to surcharges and extra fees.

Figure 3.7. Disciplined Pricing Behavior Guidelines

Be Fair and Trustworthy

Proactive   *Defensive*

| Clearly Communicate Intentions | Be Predictable. Walk the Talk | Be a Disciplined Value Pricer | React to Competitive Threats | Return to Purposeful Behavior |

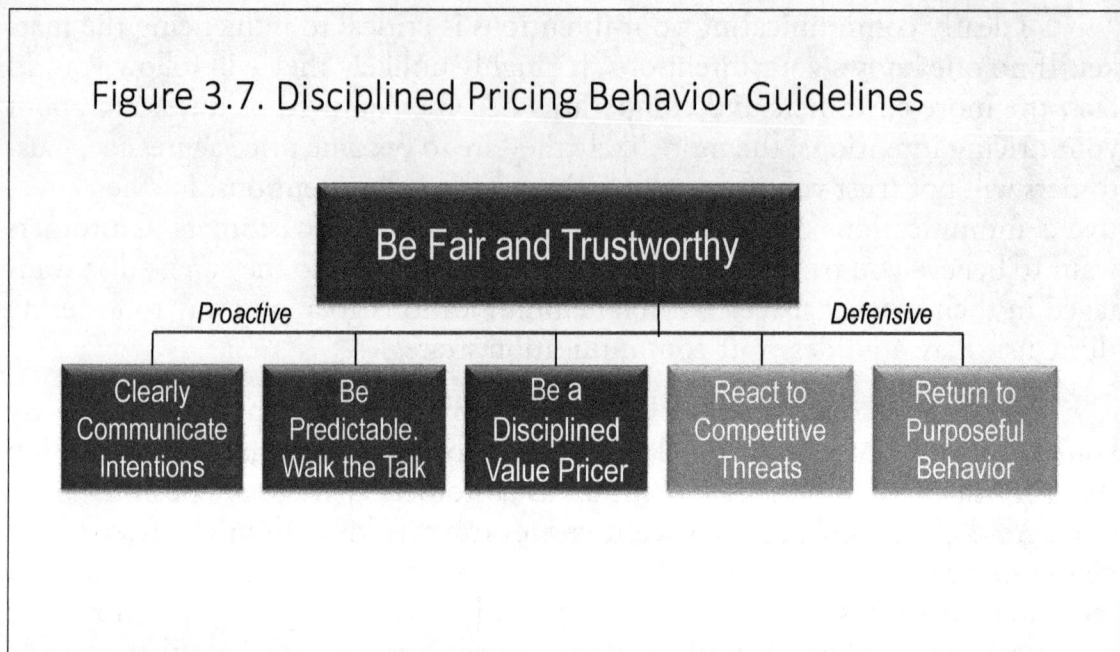

Along with these best practices, it's critical for your sales force to negotiate with…

- confidence,

- courage, and

- conviction.

I can't stress this point enough. Body language is over 70% of communication — if you don't genuinely convey confidence and conviction in your fair price, you're destined to fail many negotiations. Customers will sense your weakness and use every tactic in their arsenal to get you to discount. If you clearly don't believe your pricing position is fair, the customer certainly won't believe it's fair. You will erode trust and create a very price-aggressive customer going forward.

Further, and even more devastating, is that these customers who got you to discount will tell your competitors. It will go something like this; "X Company is not holding their price; they have given me discounts effective immediately. You also need to match these discounts if you want to retain your share with me." Now, your competitors will feel trapped and begin to lose their confidence in holding their own price. They will match the discounts with these customers, and it can get worse than that. They will also presume you are discounting your other accounts, so they will reactively discount their other customers. The competitors' other customers make sure you hear that competitors are dropping price, and this could challenge your resolve. The pricing downward spiral will pick up speed.

No matter if you are a small player in your industry or you are the largest share competitor, the practices here will work for you to influence your customers. The ability to influence your competitive base towards upward price pressure is greatest when you are in a more consolidated competitive space and you are one of the top five players. If three to five of the top competitors make up at least 50% of the market share and you have at least 5% share yourself, you will be even more successful. But if you are a small player, don't underestimate your impact on the market. If you begin a price drop for share-gain strategy, you will undermine the courage of the big players and potentially start the price war.

Case Study: *My client was an over $1 billion revenue commodity business. Their market was tight, yet a competitor was starting up a large manufacturing facility in six months which would result in a loose market. This client had recently finished a price increase with modest success. Customers had pushed back on the increase with the threat to shift to "the other competitor when their new asset started up." The pricing pressure from customers was getting even stronger. This client came to me for guidance to help them slowdown the inevitable decline in price — one they already felt had started.*

After a few days of my training and strategy workshops for their leaders and sales force, they gained the confidence, courage and conviction they needed. Rather than just slow the decline, we set a strategy to raise price again — a strategy that very much surprised them. The market was still tight, and my client had a better reputation for reliability and responsiveness than the other few large competitors. The other competitors had each experienced a few major manufacturing disruptions in the past few years that impacted their customers. Part of our strategy was to tell large 'price-only-focused' customers that we only wanted to supply them 80% of their historical volume in the coming year so we could shift our volume towards customers willing to pay a fair price — those that valued our better reliability. The result was amazing. Many of these customers immediately changed their tone, insisting they get supplied at the full historical volume level and agreeing to a price increase for the coming year. In fact, some even agreed to open the existing contract and allow the price increase to start immediately.

The overall success of this price increase was enormous and far greater than their success of the price increase they had announced less than six months earlier. In fact, the following year I worked with them for yet another successful increase. This business used the principles I'm discussing here along with the confidence they developed in our training workshop to significantly improve their business.

Leadership actions and behaviors, as perceived in the minds of sales, will impact the sales reps' confidence and conviction equally as much as will the impact of the sales compensation policies. If sales believe there are negative consequences to their reputation or pay if they risk volume to get fair price, they will not have the conviction they need for success. In turn, the customer must perceive that your company will walk away (or only supply lower value offerings) to customers unwilling to pay a fair price.

A word of advice: If you are in any way skeptical about your ability to influence the market or if the sales team does not have the confidence or skill they need for success, I strongly urge you to consider a training workshop. My pricing workshops are proven to improve your team's confidence and skill enabling leaders and sales to immediately begin making better pricing decisions. Contact me directly or go through the Professional Pricing Society to arrange online training. Alternatively, refer to my book "The Price Negotiation Playbook" for a much more in-depth discussion of the concepts presented here.

Managing Aggressive Competitors

Effectively employing the three proactive behaviors will lower the probability that you will have aggressive competitors targeting your accounts with low price. Yet, get ready, it's sure to happen at some point.

Let's focus on competitors who use excessive pricing discounts to target your accounts for share growth. If you sit back and allow them to take your share, you will embolden them to continue this tactic. If it works for them, and there are no negative repercussions, they will do it again and again. You need to thoughtfully react to these egregious situations, essentially fighting fire with fire. However, it must be done with great care, so you don't unintentionally start a price war. Thus, once you have made your point, you must quickly go back to purposeful behavior — stop retaliating against this competitor. The case study below highlights a very effective approach.

Case Study: *My client had been raising price successfully for years as had all their competitors. It was a very disciplined market; one competitor raised price and before long most other competitors followed up. That stopped during the 2009 recession. Market demand was significantly down. Competitors were panicking. One large reputable competitor approached the largest customer of my client — an account that was 100% sourced by my client. This competitor offered an unbelievable discount of 20% below market price. Fortunately, this loyal customer called my client to give them the opportunity to match this low price and retain their business. Now the panic shifted to my client's business; meeting this price drop would have an enormous negative impact to their profits.*

We quickly huddled with sales and leaders to set our plan. By the next morning, my client had a salesperson call on one of the largest loyal customers of this disruptive competitor. We were confident this customer was paying market price and not the 20% discount this competitor was offering to lure in new customers. The salesperson talked up their value and finished with a statement such as, "I know our price is about 20% higher than your current price, as we know your supplier is offering prices 20% below our price in the market, but our value is worth it."

Of course, the salesperson never expected to gain this account; they knew their value was not worth an extra 20% premium, but they also knew this customer was not receiving the enormous 20% discount their key supplier was offering new accounts. We were stirring the pot and creating some backlash to the competitor.

It turned out to be successful. This customer was likely livid with their supplier — they were their largest, loyal customer and just learned that other customers were potentially getting a much lower price. We suspect this account immediately called the competitor and demanded the same 20% discount they were offering other customers. If the competitor granted this discount, they too would take a large financial hit. What we do know is this competitor rescinded the 20% discount to my client's customer within hours. We did not have to match the discount, and this competitor stopped targeting my client's accounts with excessive discounts.

Furthermore, my client did not continue to go after other customers of this competitor. They returned to the purposeful behavior they had been employing prior to this situation.

The key points for success include:

- Act quickly and in even proportion to the competitor's action.

- Be sure they feel a negative implication to their action.

- Immediately thereafter, go back to purposeful behavior.

- Always involve leaders/sales in the planning as it's a highly effective approach but risky if done wrong.

Play 4:
Building Your Communication Plan

Don't underestimate the value of communications, both internally and externally. During times of uncertainty, good communications are more crucial. Confusion or unpredictability lead to rising anxiety and more aggressive price pressure. Follow the guidelines in Figure 4.

Internal Communications

Have you ever heard salespeople grumbling because management over-communicated to them? Probably not.

Invest the time in your communications, it will be worth it.

Sales must understand your pricing strategies (including your volume and risk tolerance) as well as your rationale. The more they buy into your rationale as well as understand it at a detailed level, the better they will be able to effectively and confidently communicate to their customers.

Provide your sales teams with:

- Written talking points

- Frequently asked (or expected) questions and appropriate responses

- Charts they can share with customers including third party projections of demand, published raw material / ingredient indexes, and economist reports — if they support your strategy rationale.

These communications should happen quickly and be frequently updated as you refine and revise your plans. Speed is important — customers will begin pressuring and questioning sales right away. If you have not provided these supports to the sales team, they will be in a very uncomfortable spot. Some sales-people, wanting to be responsive to their customers, will fill the void by answering their customers' questions with their best guesses. Imagine the implication of a response such as, "You're right, we will probably be considering price relief given the market conditions."

Not only does such a response put the salesperson in a tough spot if they must reverse that position, but it also begins to add to a more aggressive market. The customer will now feel more empowered to push you for lower price, and they will waste no time telling your competitors that your company has already said they will provide price relief. As quickly as that, you would begin to lose control in influencing the market in a more positive direction.

Sales managers should consider having their sales team role play tough situations (even if done virtually). Sales should identify their top few customers who they predict will be the toughest on price or where they believe they are most vulnerable to lose share. As a group, select two to four of these tough customer cases, and role play the discussion in front of the sales team. Invite the rest of the team to suggest other talking points or approaches.

External Communications

Customer letters, announcements or articles are not just for times of price in-creases, they are also very effective in crisis times. Effective communications and plans should include:

- Quickly and clearly communicate your position. Communicating before other suppliers will enhance the chance that your position will influence the market to a greater extent.

- Communicate in writing: Written communications are viewed as more credible than verbal communications. Third party communications, such as articles or published announcements, are interpreted as even more credible.

- Be consistent: The more customers read and consistently hear about your position, the more comfortable they will be that you are fairly and equally pricing across your customer base.

Case Study: *A large business was severely affected by the 2009 recession — market demand was down almost 40% in the first quarter of 2009. The world was a far different place than the previous three to four years when the business had increased price two to four times each year based on rising costs, tight market, and value-based adjustments. Customers were pushing hard for price relief. They were aware that raw material costs for their suppliers were declining. They wanted that reduction passed along to them and they wanted it now.*

The business knew that giving price relief was the fair thing to do and competition was likely to fold under the constant price pressure from the customer base. They feared competition would quickly discount as much as the 10% customers were demanding. Early in the 1st quarter of the year, they analyzed the situation, set their strategic plan, and communicated the points listed below to their customers:

- *Raw materials have dropped, and we will be passing along price relief to our customers. This relief will come in the second quarter. When we increased price in the past, due to our raw materials rising, we took months to pass along these increases to you.*

- *Our price drops will be on products A, B, and C as these are the products materially affected by our lower-priced raw materials.*

- *Our price decline will be in the 3%–5% range depending on the product. Our increases over the past few years have been based on a combination of reasons going well beyond raw material increases. Some increases were based on value and others on basic inflationary costs that are not eroding.*

An additional point was also shared internally and with the specific customers affected:

- *Some customers will receive less price relief than the stated 3%–5% if they had not fully accepted our price increases in the past or their price is noticeably below target.*

This clear communication was effective in slowing the speed and the magnitude of the price decline. It demonstrated openness and fairness to both the customers and their own business. It also lowered the confusion and anxiety both internally and externally.

Figure 4. Building A Communication Plan

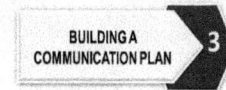

Engage Sales	• Sales must understand your strategy & the rationale. • Consider 'role play' for holding price.
Information Packages	• Provide sales with talking points, frequently asked questions & responses, charts they can show to customers...
External Messaging	• Consider customer letters, articles, etc. to ensure customers understand your position & believe it's evenly applied.
On-going Updates	• As market dynamics change, update your communication plan.

BUILDING A COMMUNICATION PLAN 3

Play 5:
Creating Tighter Disciplined Deal Approvals

For anyone with training in disaster crisis management (e.g., a hurricane, a terrorist attack), you know command and control rule. This is not the time for great debate, the challenging of decisions, and wide-spread freedom of decisions. It is a time to pull out your crisis plans and follow the chain of command in a disciplined manner. Your Pricing Crisis Preparedness Plan should include the time-tested successful practices as illustrated in Figure 5.

In market downturns, you need to tighten your discipline on both your deal price approvals and your policy adherence. This may seem counterintuitive. Sales may argue that they need more price flexibility as the market is more competitive — they need to be able to discount deeper and faster in response to this changing market. If every decision was a one-off decision that stood alone, didn't affect the future aggressiveness of the market/competitors, and didn't contribute to a possible faster decline of the overall market price then that would be a fair argument. However, that is not the case and our focus here is on how to prevent or slow a market price decline.

If you are embracing the recommendations discussed in earlier chapters and committed to proactively influencing the market, you will need to think strategically. You must weigh how each deal decision supports or detracts from your overall strategy. Is it more important to optimize a single deal or to optimize your total business? Of course, the total business is the correct response, but in the heat of the moment it is all too easy to focus on the immediate deal in hand. The big picture gets momentarily forgotten.

Any deal, looked at in isolation, could appear to have a valid argument for discounting over and above normal guardrails. Sales teams, by the very nature of their role, lean towards deal by deal decisions. Further, they are typically compensated based on their own results — not the results of the total business. This drives the short-term deal by deal focus. On the other hand, marketing/business/

pricing roles, by their very nature, are tasked to take a longer-term view that optimizes the full business. At times, this creates some tension between the functions, yet it is a necessary tension. The balance and tension of strategic longer-term thinking with the excellence of execution is a good thing.

Given the potential enormous price pressure your sales teams will face, you will need a tightly disciplined approval process. This process will need to be…

- Strategic: Assess each decision's impact on the market and its impact on your overall strategy.

- Principle-based: Discount based on specific principles that guide all similar situations (e.g., For relationship buyers with margins over x%, we will allow 60-day temporary price relief of up to Y%).

- Timely: Make expeditious decisions. When the market is loose, and your competitors are hungry for your volume, slow decisions can cost you the deal.

If your business does some of the strategy-setting frameworks discussed in this playbook, (e.g., differential management discussed in Play 7), you will have developed the principles that should guide your decisions. As you go through the crisis, continue to evaluate your earlier strategies and tactics regarding the customer/competitor dynamics. If you see new patterns emerging, update your principle-based pricing guidance.

A good test for the approval team to utilize is to ensure that for every deeper discount or waiving of a policy, there is a written principle or policy that allows this decision. If not, what principle could be written, and should this new principle be added to the list that governs all future decisions? If there is no principle, existing or anticipated, don't discount.

Adherence to policies can be difficult to measure and control unless you have strong professional price management systems. Consider taking all rights away from sales to waive policies such as extra fees for expedited shipments, special analyses or late payments.

Consistent with your guiding principle of being fair to both the customer and your business, if your company should drop the ball (e.g., shipped poor quality, shipped late, etc.) there should be no penalty for the customer. However, if you're finding a pattern of waiving fees due to your company dropping the ball too frequently, your policy might possibly be written in a way that is not fair to your company and should be modified. Ordering and shipping policies should be carefully reviewed and aligned to your internal capabilities. For example;

- Don't allow customers to order with only two days advance notice if you can't consistently meet this timeline. If this policy results in you paying expedited shipping costs, or shipping small, less than economical lots, then modify your policy.

Having tight deal / policy approval processes may even help your sales team. They can potentially use this in their negotiations to counter price pressure. For example, "Given the financial strain on our company at this time, approvals for discounts require management approval — an approval they're not likely to provide."

Figure 5. Creating a Tighter-Disciplined Deal Approval Process

Avoid Price War	• Every discount has the unintentional consequence of creating more aggressive customers and competitors. Tread carefully.
Deal Approval Process	• Shift to a tighter 'principle-led' price approval process. • It signals to the market your conviction to hold to fair price.
Policy Adherence	• Hold rigidly to surcharge/fee policies. Don't waive. • Consider removing sales from the decision.
Fairness	• Fairness to you & your customers should guide decisions. • It's not your role to bail out customers at your expense.

Play 6:
Forming a Crisis Management Team and Process

These are dynamic times with considerable uncertainty. The strategies and tactics you set initially, based on your best predictions of the market, aren't likely to be the best actions throughout the crisis. Dynamics will change for the better or the worst and you need to react quickly. Certainly, as you begin to see a recovery of the crisis, you may want to take far different strategies in a timely manner. As shown in Figure 6, you will need a small team governing the strategies, tactics, processes, and communications.

Consider one resource fully or significantly dedicated to monitoring and managing the pricing crisis. This may be a pricing manager. This individual should report to a steering team for guidance or intervention. The steering team could well be your business team or a subset of the business team.

The frequency of which this team meets will be distinctly different than during normal times. In the initial days, it might meet daily, then shift to weekly with ad hoc meetings for any major development. Depending on the length of the crisis, it may eventually shift towards a monthly session.

A key aspect of the crisis processes will be to maintain a good understanding of the changing market dynamics. To aid this, I strongly encourage you to hold "pulse-check" meetings with your sales force.

Sales Pulse-Check Meetings

A pulse-check meeting is a roughly 15-minute interaction with the sales team. It's an informal discussion guided by this framework:

- What changes are you seeing in the market with your customers?

- What new competitive intelligence are you seeing?

- What new challenges are you facing?

- What help do you need from leadership?

This is also a time for the leader to provide any new guidance to the sales team. I'd suggest holding these meetings once a week initially and as things begin to settle down, shift to bi-weekly check-ins.

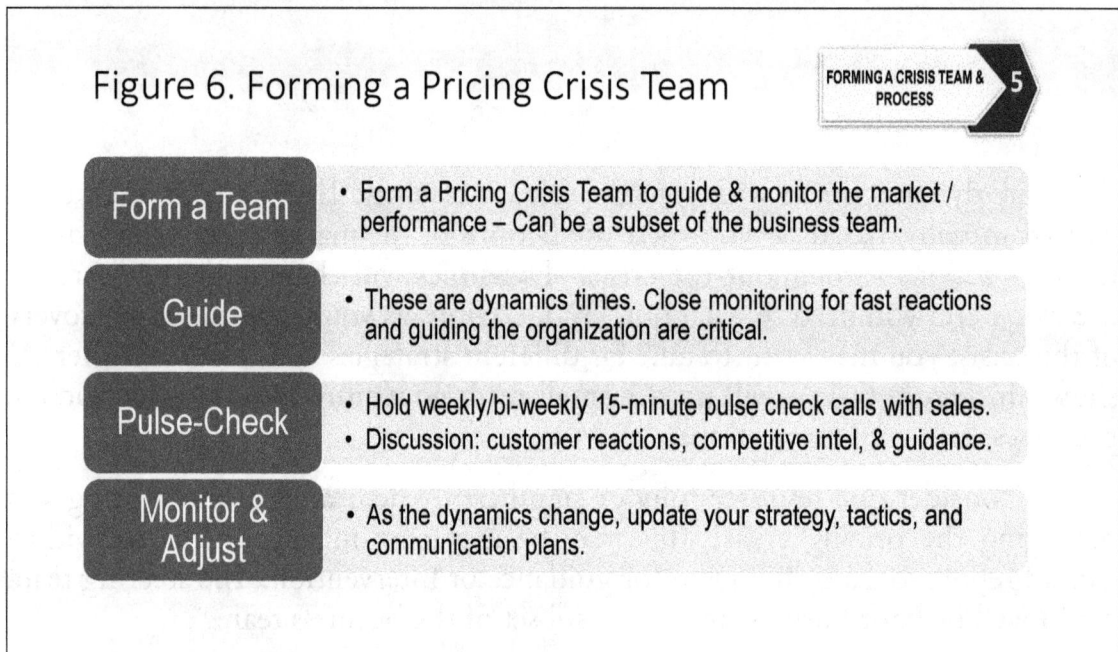

Figure 6. Forming a Pricing Crisis Team

FORMING A CRISIS TEAM & PROCESS 5

Form a Team
- Form a Pricing Crisis Team to guide & monitor the market / performance – Can be a subset of the business team.

Guide
- These are dynamics times. Close monitoring for fast reactions and guiding the organization are critical.

Pulse-Check
- Hold weekly/bi-weekly 15-minute pulse check calls with sales.
- Discussion: customer reactions, competitive intel, & guidance.

Monitor & Adjust
- As the dynamics change, update your strategy, tactics, and communication plans.

Play 7:
Adapting to Different Customer Buyer Types

There are four different customer buyer types that dominate the B2B space. Nearly all businesses have at least the first three of the four types listed below:

- The Price Buyer

- The Value Buyer

- The Relationship (Loyal) Buyer

- The Convenience Buyer

Differentiation, in your offering and your price, for each buyer type is your best strategy. You have diverse pricing power with each type, and you should be treating each type accordingly to optimize your price and your volume. To treat them differently, you must first identify your customer's buying type. That is not always as easy as it sounds because many purchasing agents intentionally present their companies as price buyers when in fact they are not.

Let's imagine that we are watching fans going to a professional sporting event in an arena. We could categorize them into four groups:

- The price buyer: Likely people with limited funds, such as college students, who would buy the cheapest seats even if that meant sitting in the upper bleachers.

- The value buyer: Likely young families, who are financially stable but with limited discretionary funds. They would carefully consider the seat choice / price trade-offs and choose a mid-range seat. They would pay a small premium for a better seat.

- The relationship buyer: These are the season ticket holders. They are willing to pay for the best seats.

- The convenience buyer: They may be companies that are hosting a customer event. They want the best and they want it easy. They are relatively unconcerned about the price and will pay a premium.

In the B2B world, it's a little harder to spot the buyer type than you can in consumer markets, largely because B2B purchasing agents are trained and/or skilled at misleading you to think, "it's all about price." Here is some guidance for handling each type of buyer.

A word of caution: The buyer type does not necessarily refer to the purchasing agent's behavior. It refers to the business's buying behavior, particularly how they make their buying decisions. Frequently, the purchasing agent is not the decision maker or at least not the sole decision maker. The purchasing agent may use negotiation tactics such as pretending to be a price buyer or pretending they have full decision rights for their company to bolster their negotiating power. Be on the lookout for these misleading approaches.

Price Buyer

Price buyers are all about price, price, and price. They will gladly use all your services (and may even be among your higher cost-to-serve customers) but only if they are free. Given a choice between lower price and extra features, services, and special customer experience, they will choose a lower price.

They aren't loyal to you unless you have the lowest price. They shop around for competitive bids and they will switch suppliers for lower price. Price buyers often have two or three key suppliers and they will play one supplier off the others to drive price down.

The purchasing agent is typically the sole decision maker in their company, and they make fast decisions. It's easy to make fast decisions if you're just comparing prices.

Your pricing power is low with price buyers unless they are buying an important product – one they might view as risky if the quality or reliability is not good. For these important products, your pricing power jumps up from low to mediocre.

Pricing Policies and Tactics

The key tips for selling to price buyers include:

- Avoid discounting faster or deeper than your business is doing for their full customer base.

- If their price is already low, relative to other customers their size, seriously consider walking away from this business before discounting further.

- If you do discount, do so by providing a lower value offering. Either a lower value product or remove services.

- Do charge them extra fees for any requests or services beyond the basic product.

- Don't make any firm long-term price commitments; retain the ability to raise their price if the market rebounds.

Value Buyer

The value buyer sits somewhere between the price buyer and the relationship buyer. They value some of your features but not all. They tend towards loyalty but are also weighing their options. Value buyers are the hardest to identify because many of them pretend to be price buyers. They want you to believe they only care about price; they pretend they aren't willing to pay for your value or your value is no different than the other suppliers. They do this because it works; they successfully get salespeople to discount lower than necessary.

Despite their tough talk about price, price, price, they are surprisingly loyal. They are quite price sensitive — it is important to them — but they will pay a reasonable premium for the few things that they value.

These buyers shop around for competitive bids yet don't easily switch suppliers unless there is a compelling price/value trade-off. Value buyers often have two key suppliers both with reasonable share.

Unlike price buyers, the purchasing agent of a value buyer is generally not the decision maker (or at least not the sole decision maker). They need to get approval to switch suppliers from an owner, manager, or user in the business such as the person/group that uses/receives your value. As a result, they are slow decision makers. Not only do they need to involve multiple people, but they also need to assess the trade-offs between price and different features/services of the suppliers.

Your pricing power is surprisingly good with value buyers. It's better than you likely think.

Pricing Policies and Tactics

The key tips for selling to value buyers include:

- Offer them options: a high-value offer at a high price versus a low value offer at a low price (may be even a mid-value, mid-price option). When designing the low-value offer, attempt to remove the feature/service that you believe they especially value. If they are interested in this lower-value offer, then they are likely a price buyer. However, if they insist that they need that extra feature/service, you know you have value, thus you have pricing power.

- Help them make comparisons between your offering options and the competitors' offer. They value this guidance.

- If their price is already low, relative to other customers their size, hold their price until it comes in line with other customers even if your business is broadly dropping price.

- Do charge them extra fees for any requests or services beyond the offer option they chose.

Relationship Buyer

The relationship buyers are often your favorite customers. They appreciate all your value, especially the extra attention, hand-holding services, and responsiveness. They want to feel important to you.

They are very loyal and rarely shop around. The business is yours to lose. They care about price but will pay a premium for your extra value. They trust you to treat them fairly.

Relationship buyers often have a primary supplier or even a sole supplier. If they have a back-up supplier, this competitor will have a much smaller share. The buyer will not have the same loyal relationship with the competitor.

The decision maker is probably a business manager or owner, not the procurement resource.

Your pricing power is very strong with relationship buyers provided you continue to treat them well and fairly.

Pricing Policies and Tactics

The key tips for selling to relationship buyers include:

- Offer them a high-value option: one with the extra service they appreciate.

- Don't discount. These should be among your highest-priced accounts as you are offering them the highest value.

- Make them feel special. Use dedicated salespeople or even dedicated customer service or technical service representatives if that makes sense for your business. If they are large, establish a relationship between your leaders and their leaders.

- If they are not among your highest margin accounts, assess whether you have been underpricing them in the past. If so, this may be a time to correct your pricing by discounting less to them should your business begin providing price relief.

- If they are paying fair price, avoid nickel-and-diming them with a lot of extra fees unless it involves high cost-to-serve elements – ones they would reasonably expect to pay extra for.

- If they are under severe financial stress, and they have historically been paying a fair premium, you might selectively decide to provide temporary price relief in exchange for some longer-term contract or additional volume.

Convenience Buyer

Convenience buyers aren't always prevalent in many B2B businesses; yet, businesses with store fronts (e.g., construction equipment and parts stores for installer/contractors) may have a large segment of these buyer types. Convenience buyers select their suppliers because they are easy to do business with and fast to deliver. They are not price focused and will pay a premium especially if they are calling in an emergency.

They have their go-to supplier that they continue to use if that supplier continues to be fast and easy to work with.

The decision maker is probably the purchasing agent. They make fast decisions, generally just buying from their 'go-to' supplier.

Your pricing power is very strong provided you continue to be fast and easy to do business with.

Pricing Policies and Tactics

The key tips for selling to convenience buyers include:

- Don't discount.

- Charge an extra premium for expedited or emergency orders.

- Be fast and easy to work with.

During a crisis, you may find that customers who previously were loyal and who valued you as a supplier, begin to act like price buyers. In fact, if they are under tremendous financial strain, they may not have a choice. They may reluctantly be forced to shift to a low-price supplier. It's also possible that you have price or value buyers shift to more loyal buyers if they believe they will need your support throughout the crisis.

The governing principle for all types of buyers is: If they want the extra value you deliver, then they must pay a premium. If they aren't willing to pay for all your value, you must offer a lower value option or walk away.

Principled-based Differential Management

Designing a principled-based segmentation, mapping your customers into the appropriate segment, then setting differential policies and guidance for each segment may be an easier and more effective approach to getting buy-in and understanding from your sales force.

Design your Segments

Design a four-box segmentation based on the attractiveness of your customers to your business and your attractiveness to your customers as shown in Figure 7.

Figure 7. Differential Price Management

CUSTOMER ATTRACTIVENESS (Revenue, Margin, Strategic Fit)	DEFEND & STRENGHTEN	DELIGHT & SELECTIVELY GROW
High	• Lee Industries • Distributor B • • •	• ACME Products • Jones Inc. • Smith LLC • Best Polymers •
	IMPROVE & TAKE RISKS	CAPTURE MORE VALUE
Low	• Johnson Inc. • Lee Products • Jurgen Plastics • •	• Bob's Shop • Hanson LLC • • •
	We are DISADVANTAGED	We are ADVANTAGED

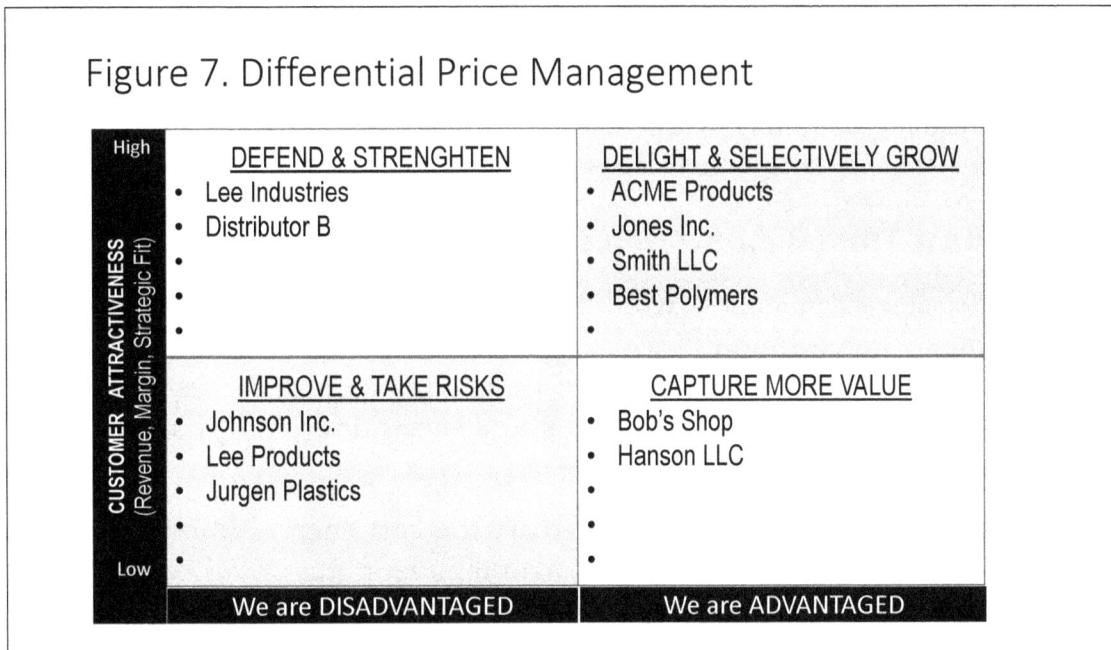

The X-axis: Customers should be grouped into one of two groups:

• We are advantaged: These customers are likely to choose us over competitors even at a slight premium price. These customers may value all or part of our product portfolio, customer experience, or services. They may have a deep relationship with our salesperson, or they may be located close to our facilities.

• We are disadvantaged: These customers are more likely to choose a competitor especially if we insist on a price premium. These customers are likely price buyers, located near a competitor's facilities, have a deep relationship with a competitor or they prefer a competitor's product portfolio, customer experience or services.

The Y-axis: Calculate this axis using your customer's revenue and margin percent with you (the year just prior to the crisis).

• The upper quadrant should consist of your largest revenue customers who also have a good/okay margin percent when compared to other large customers and your target margin percent. Include mid-sized revenue accounts that have high margins. Do not include customers because you 'think and hope' to grow with them someday or just because they are in your top 10% of revenue. They must earn their way into this quadrant. You could also consider strategic fit. If any of these customers are in markets that are not strategic to you or products that you will be discontinuing, you may opt to downrate them to the lower quadrant.

- The lower quadrant is all other customers: large customers with low margins, mid-sized accounts with average to low margins, and your small accounts.

Set Segment Treatment Strategies

Treatment strategies and tactics will be different during crises times than during normal times. They will also differ by business. The example shown in Figure 7.1 is just an illustration and not meant to be adopted in its exact form for all businesses. Each quadrant should have a unique overriding strategy and different tactics. Overriding strategies might be:

- **Delight & Selectively Grow:** These are the customers you love, and they love you. Continue to build and maintain your great relationship and/or value delivery. Cautiously grow your share if you can do so without major competitor backlash.

- **Defend & Strengthen Position:** While these customers are attractive to you, you're not so special to them. There is a real threat of them shifting their share to another competitor. Consider actions to strengthen your position with them and defend your share.

- **Capture More Value:** These customers really value you but probably are not paying sufficient price. You want to improve the profitability of these accounts through lowering services, changing policies, or charging extra fees for special requests.

- **Improve & Take Risks:** These are likely your least favorite customers and they are fairly indifferent to you. They are probably price buyers that have successfully negotiated a very low price with you. You should improve the profitability of these accounts through holding/raising price, reducing services and adding fees for all special requests even if it means you risk losing their business.

Figure 7.1. Differential Price Management - In a Crisis

CUSTOMER ATTRACTIVENESS (Revenue, Margin, Strategic Fit)	DEFEND & STRENGHTEN RELATIONSHIP	DELIGHT & SELECTIVELY GROW
High	• Lock in with contracts.	• Quantify/communicate value; keep premium.
	• Modify offer/price if needed.	• Offer temporary price concessions, if needed, linked to long-term relationship or lower value.
	• Meet competitive prices to retain.	• Adjust offering to evolving needs.
	• Don't nickel & dime them.	• Provide high touch / build the relationship.
	• Strengthen relationships / Provide high touch.	• Don't nickel & dime them.
	• Communicate your value / Fix value gaps.	• Cautiously grow w/ cumulative volume rebates.
	• Offer extra value: help through crisis?	
	IMRPOVE & TAKE RISKS	**CAPTURE MORE VALUE**
	• Resist dropping price / risk share loss.	• Communicate value & resist price drops.
	• Walk away if consistently low priced.	• Selectively risk volume to hold price.
	• Lessen touch: No services, inside seller...	• Eliminate low-value, high cost services.
	• Add surcharges for every extra.	• Lessen touch slightly: fewer visits, lower priority...
	• Stop waiving fees: cancellation, late payment...	• Add surcharges for high cost-to-serve items.
	• Test new pricing structures/policies.	• Stop waiving fees: cancellation, late payments...
Low	• Stop or limit contracts unless price openers.	• Add price openers to contracts (e.g., 90 days).
	We are DISADVANTAGED	**We are ADVANTAGED**

Play 8:
Price Pressure Conversations

Price pressure will ramp up and sales needs to be skilled and confident in handling these discussions. This four-step process which is summarized in Figure 8 should guide your customer discussions:

- Defuse the situation and redirect the conversation.

- Uncover changing price and non-price needs.

- Identify the customer needs-based buyer type and test offering options.

- Influence and align on the deal.

These guidelines apply to existing customers you know well. You should probe deeper on their needs if they are not known well to you.

Figure 8: Price Pressure Conversation in a Crisis

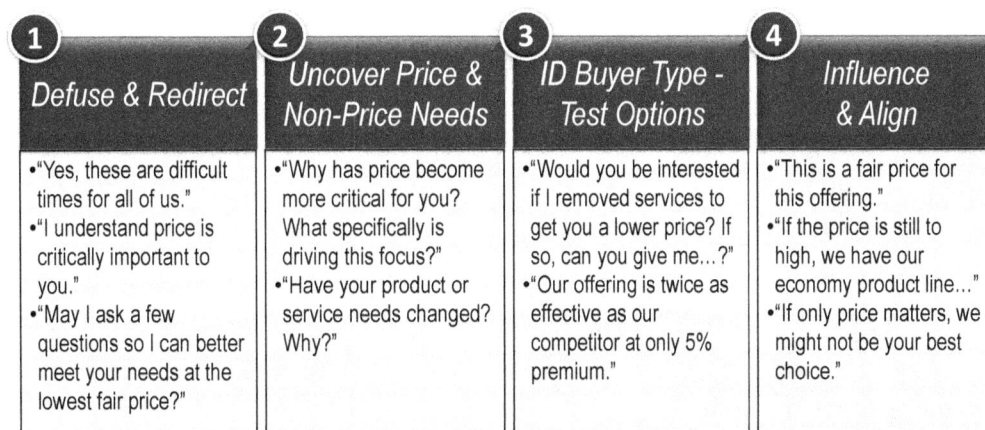

1 Defuse & Redirect	**2** Uncover Price & Non-Price Needs	**3** ID Buyer Type - Test Options	**4** Influence & Align
•"Yes, these are difficult times for all of us." •"I understand price is critically important to you." •"May I ask a few questions so I can better meet your needs at the lowest fair price?"	•"Why has price become more critical for you? What specifically is driving this focus?" •"Have your product or service needs changed? Why?"	•"Would you be interested if I removed services to get you a lower price? If so, can you give me...?" •"Our offering is twice as effective as our competitor at only 5% premium."	•"This is a fair price for this offering." •"If the price is still to high, we have our economy product line..." •"If only price matters, we might not be your best choice."

Step 1. Defuse and Redirect

Show empathy for the tough times we all face and very clearly acknowledge that you understand pricing is critically important to them. Let them know you want to ask a few questions so you can provide them the offering that best meets their needs given their price concerns. Get their okay to hold off on the price discussion for a few minutes. Assure them you **will** come back to their price concerns with potential solutions after you get further information.

Step 2. Uncover Changing Needs—Price and Non-Price

This is a time to listen and learn. Avoid moving quickly to price concessions until you have a deeper understanding of their current (probably changing) needs.

Pricing Needs: Uncover their rationale for the reason price is now so important to them. Don't assume you know the answer to this question. Their response may well help to uncover a need that you can solve in a different way than just low price. As an example, you might have different solutions if their response relates to cash flow constraints versus total cost of operation issues or if they are incented to reduce supplier costs.

Non-Price Needs: Probe to understand if any of their non-price needs are changing (they may no longer be willing to pay for extra value). If they are giving up value they used to buy, probe to quantify the implications of this decision. For example, "If you shift to this lower value gasket, the life of the gasket is shorter. What is the cost or penalty to your company for a gasket failure?"

Unstated Needs: Probe further into any favorable services, payment terms, or value you provide to test the importance of these with this customer.

Step 3. Identify the Buyer Type & Test Options

You likely already have identified the buyer type, yet you need to reassess if this still holds true as the crisis may have caused them to change their behaviors. Some customers who traditionally pay a premium for your extra value may not be willing or able to afford this any longer. While on the other hand, value buyers may become relationship buyers if they perceive a strong need for your support through the crisis.

Test Offering Options and Buyer Type: If you perceive the customer's needs are changing or they are likely a value buyer, then test different offering/price options with them. Identify what you believe might be one or two of their biggest needs, then explore offerings that remove these needs to get at a lower price. If the buyer insists on having those needs included or insists on comparing the price with or without these needs included, then there is high likelihood this is a value buyer. If so, you have good pricing power. The conversation might go something like this: *"Would you be interested in options that exclude short lead times and technical service if I were able to provide you a lower price?"*

You are not necessarily trying to put forward the best offering for them yet or even necessarily a real option. You are just trying to test their conviction to 'lowest price is the only thing that matters.' Once you establish this answer, you are ready to explore real options to find the win-win solution for the customer and you.

Help them compare the trade-offs between your own offering options as well as potential competitor options. If you are providing the concession of a lower-priced offer, this is an ideal time to ask for a concession from them.

Take the time to prepare your options, especially the price point. Break the negotiation into a second session if you feel that would be beneficial. This break could potentially give you time to talk beyond the purchasing agent to the users who value your offering. Perhaps ask these users to advocate on your behalf.

Step 4. Influence and Align

At this point, you are ready to close the deal. You are essentially aligned on the offering and its value and probably even the price. However, the buyer may make another run at getting some price concession.

The Soft Push: The buyer has turned friendlier and more open to discussion. They inquire if there isn't something else you could do to reduce their price just a little further. They test your conviction and play on your relationship. This is the time to hold firm—to ensure them this is your fair and appropriate price.

The Hard Push: The buyer may try to delay the decision in the hopes of making you nervous thus undermining your confidence. They may imply they will be exploring other suppliers. Counter their pushback by 1) assuring them your price is fair for that offer, and 2) you're committed to being compensated fairly. Such as:

- If you need an even lower price, we can offer you our 'economy-line' products (e.g., lower value product).

- If price is the only thing that matters, we may not be the best supplier for you.

- It is our company's intention during this crisis to align our supply with customers who value what we bring to the table and to more strongly support these customers as we come out of this downturn. (This works well if they think they will need your company post-crisis).

Play 9:
Making Smart Discount Decisions

There are four main reasons why customers may push back on price in a crisis:

- **Fairness in Your Value/Price:** In their eyes, your price is too high versus competitors who may be dropping price, or they are no longer willing or able to pay for your extra value.

- **Fairness versus Other Customers**: They worry that you are giving better prices to other customers. They want to feel fairly treated.

- **Tactic, Tactic, Tactic:** It's a key tactic to test your conviction and your confidence. They are testing to see if you believe in the fairness of your own price. They are throwing spaghetti on the wall to see if it sticks.

- **Fairness in Your Rationale:** They don't understand your rationale for holding (or even increasing) your price in this downturn, thus they question the fairness of your price.

If you believe in the fairness of your price, then your confidence, conviction, and good communications go a long way to convincing the buyer s/he is fairly treated. Of the reasons listed above, only one is a valid reason to consider dropping price — fairness in your value/price. Consider the following:

- ***Strategic / structural price drop:*** If the price pressure is broad, determine your position strategically. Dropping price might be the fair thing to do. Alternatively, consciously decide to risk or walk away from volume.

- ***Deal by deal:*** Consider a lower-value, lower-priced option or walking away from these accounts if their price expectation is lower than the business's strategic decision.

During normal times, typically 90% of price pushback is not because your price is wrong — it's a tactic or a result of insufficient communications. During a crisis, that 90% will be lower but probably not dramatically so. Buyer's will feel that they are in the power seat in loose markets and double down on shaking your confidence.

Price-Drop Decision Checklist

The following framework will guide you on whether to discount price or hold. It can be used at a strategic level (e.g., for a full market, product line) or deal by deal.

There are eleven questions to consider as shown in Figure 9. Your responses will fall into one of three categories; favorable to drop, unfavorable to drop or cautionary (straddling the line between unfavorable and favorable). If most of your responses fall in the unfavorable to drop category, you should consider holding your price. Likewise, if the majority land in the 'favorable to drop' then consider providing price relief. If your responses don't dominate one category, use your best judgement yet place more emphasis on the customer buying behavior and the market fairness questions.

Figure 9. Price Drop Decision Framework

	Favorable to drop	Unfavorable to Drop
1. Why?	Competitive threat	Buyer asks / share gain
2. Consequence of not dropping?	Big share lost	No / little share loss
3. Which competitor?	Large / reliable *(gain: New/ small/ not local)*	New / small / not local *(share gain: large / reliable)*
4. Customer's buying behavior?	Price buyer/ not loyal	Loyal
5. Product differentiation	Commodity	Unique
6. Customer needs changing?	Lower needs	The same / higher
7. Relative account price / margin?	High	Same / low
8. Price/volume trade-off?	Volume lose hurts profits	Price lose hurts profits
9. Competitive reaction?	Will not know or react	Will know / will react
10. Competitive offering?	Better	Same / worse
11. Market fairness?	Loose market / less costs	Tight market / rising costs

1. **Why are you considering a drop?**

   Favorable to drop: Competitors are lowering prices or to stimulate increased market size

   Unfavorable: To meet customer desire/expectation, to gain share or to pull sales forward into the next financial quarter/year

2. **What will happen if you don't drop price?**

   Favorable to drop: Likely large share loss

   Unfavorable: No or small share loss

3. **To whom will you lose the share?**

   Favorable to drop: One of the top suppliers

   Unfavorable: A new, small, or low-end competitor or an opportunistic importer

4. **What is the customer's buying behavior? Is it changing?**

   Favorable to drop: A price buyer—not loyal, switches suppliers often

   Unfavorable: Loyal relationship or value buyer to you or to one of your competitors

5. **Is your product differentiated?**

   Favorable to drop: Undifferentiated or commodity products

   Unfavorable: Slightly to unique products

6. **Are customer needs changing? Is your value proposition clear?**

   Favorable to drop: Competitors are closing the gap, the customer is no longer willing/able to pay for our value

   Unfavorable: Your value is clear, and the customer needs this value.

7. **What is the account price or contribution margin?**

   Favorable to drop: High or higher than similar sized customers

   Unfavorable: The same or lower than similar sized customers

8. **What is the break-even volume?**

   Favorable to drop: Contribution dollars increase. Profits from retaining (or gaining) volume more than offset the profit loss from dropping the price.

Unfavorable: Contribution dollars from retaining (or gaining) volume will not offset the profit loss from price decline. Total profitability will decline.

9. **Will there be a competitive reaction or spillover to other customers?**

    Favorable to drop: Competitors and other customers are unlikely to know of your price drop, so no spillover effect is expected. Competitors are unlikely to drop price even if they know.

    Unfavorable: Your price drop is likely visible to competitors and/or other customers. Spillover is likely. Competitors will probably react with even further price drops.

10. **What is the competitive offering, including value, terms, volume, etc. compared to your offering?**

    Favorable to drop: Comparable to or better than yours. Competitor is a large, reliable supplier with a sustainable offer.

    Unfavorable: Lower value offering. Competitor is an untried or potentially unreliable supplier. Competitor is only offering a one-time buy or a short-term offer. Buyer is unwilling to show you, or provide details of, the competitive bid he/she has asked you to match.

11. **Do you have a solid rationale for holding/increasing price given these market conditions? How did you justify increases in the past?**

    Favorable to drop: No solid rationale for holding/increasing price. Past increases were done based on your rising raw material costs which are now dropping. The customer volume is increasing significantly.

    Unfavorable: There is a solid rationale for holding/increasing price. Customer is below average on profitability. Customer volume is dropping. Your raw material costs are increasing. Your offering has higher value than that of competitors.

How to Effectively Drop Price

If you're considering strategic level, broad based discounts, revisit the strategies listed in play 3.

For deal by deal decisions, if it looks like dropping price might be the smart move, first consider these preemptive moves before the price-drop options that follow:

- Go beyond the buyer and reach out to the users of your products or the organization that gets the value from your offer. Play on their fears and uncertainties. Recruit these users/value receivers to advocate on your behalf to their buyer.

- If the situation is in response to an excessively low-priced competitor bid, quickly try to retaliate against this competitor (per guidance in Play 3) in the hopes of having them stop their aggressive pricing.

The following tactics may help you to minimize or delay the discount as well as minimize creating a more aggressive market for future deals.

Tactic 1: Value Pricing

If you have additional value over the competitive offer, don't drop your price as far.

- Consider all elements of product, quality, service, brand, reliability, and relationship value.

- Consider factors such as switching cost and/or perceived risk of switching.

- Get all the details of the competitive offer you're being asked to match.

Tactic 2: Take Something Away

Discount like a value pricer. Take something away.

- Examples: Less services, longer lead times, shorter payment terms, shorter contract commitment, no custom products, no technical support, freight excluded, weekday delivery only, ship to one location only, shift to make-to-order versus off-the-shelf, limit the volume at this lower price.

Tactic 3: Get Something of Value

Consider asking for something of value for your company.

- Examples: More share or volume, longer contract commitment (if this is an attractive account), first right to bid on their future applications, access to performance data on your products versus competitive products, access to decision makers, a modified formula pricing structure, endorsements or price openers in the contract

Tactic 4: Add More Value

Consider adding value that appeals to the customer rather than dropping price.

- Examples: Additional services, extension of warranties or guarantees, shorter lead times, co-branding, six-month exclusivity on new products, first rights to test your new products, credit, training sessions, financing options

Tactic 5: Temporary, Select, or Delayed Incentives

Offer time or volume limited options as well as delaying the discount.

- Temporary or Select Examples: Temporary 90-day discount or rebate, 60-day trial period at X% discount, only X tons.

- Delayed Examples: Announce a discount is coming in two months or after X units are bought. Offer a rebate after the customer buys Y units.

Tactic 6: Incumbent Value

Being the incumbent supplier is often worth a slight premium. Customers avoid the risk and hassles of changing suppliers.

- Examples: Minimum 2%-3% higher than an alternate supplier of like reputation or minimum 5% higher for less established supplier

Tactic 7: Secondary Supplier Position

If you are not the primary supplier, don't be pushed into matching the price of the primary supplier. Your price should be higher if they are buying less from you.

- Example: Price several percent higher if you have noticeably less volume than the primary supplier.

Tactic 8: Threats to Reduce your Share

If the customer threatens to drop your share by ~20%, consider 1) rebates only on their last increment of purchases or 2) walking away from this volume while raising their price slightly.

- Reduction on last increment of business example: First 100 tons at $2/ton and next 10 tons at $1.90/ton or use cumulative volume rebates.

- Walk Away example: Walk away from this portion of the business but also raise price 2%–3%, based on their lower volume. (The increased price will offset much of the profit loss from the volume decline.)

- End-user customer-specific rebate example: Rebate only on portion of product that your customer sells through to low-value, end-user applications.

Tactic 9: Adjust Rebates or Volume Discounts

If you do lose volume, remove or adjust pre-existing volume related rebates or discounts that were based on their larger buy. During the negotiation, let them know this is one of the consequences of lower volume.

- Example: Shift from something like 5% discount from list price to 5% rebate if purchases hit a quarterly minimum of X.

Tactic 10: Consider Offering Two or Three Choices

Offer choices to stimulate value discussions and better meet customer needs. Examples:

- Low value/low price: Core products only, six-weeks lead-time, full truckload and no service

- Mid value/mid-price: Most products, one-week lead time, technical service

- High value/high price: All products, two-day lead time, technical service including a 24-hour hotline

Tactic 11: Reduce Price Only on At-risk Products/Markets

Avoid the trap of thinking you need to reduce all products or across all markets if the volume risk is isolated to one product or market.

- Examples: 5% on commodity grades ABC; 0% on unique grades DEF

Tactic 12: Discount Less Than Expected in Unfavorable Market Conditions

- Example: Reduce discounts to customers who didn't fully accept past increases or who have a price below floor price.

Play 10:

The DuPont Story through the Great Recession of 2009

Let me set the stage for DuPont's story through the great recession of 2009.

In 2004 I began leading the corporate pricing transformation for the DuPont Company. It started at a time when our company had no pricing group, no pricing analysts, no pricing managers, and no corporate marketing and sales organization. Essentially, DuPont had no pricing competency. None. And not surprisingly, our pricing performance was quite weak. For example, many of our businesses had not successfully increased prices in years despite many attempts to do so, while other businesses had not even attempted it even when increases were justified.

For over a dozen years (or as long as I could get data), the company's variable profit margins were continually eroding over ten percentage points—a hard pill to swallow for a company that prides itself on its premium products. But in that era, volume and revenue growth ruled, while any focus on pricing took a back seat.

Fortunately, in 2004, DuPont's CEO Chad Holiday recognized the value of smart pricing. In fact, he made it the top priority of our newly created Corporate Marketing and Sales organization. Our initial pricing goal and my number one objective was to stop our margin erosion and build pricing competency across DuPont.

Despite our CEO's strong support, our pricing journey was a tough one. At the time, DuPont had roughly 60 business units grouped into 16 strategic business organizations. Each strategic business organization had autonomy for running its businesses. Rarely did Corporate impose specific activity on the businesses.

To get started, we shifted 15 internal business, marketing, and general process consultants into pricing consultants — albeit untrained, unskilled pricing consultants. Thus, there we were in our new corporate group — one that could only influence businesses but had no decision-making rights — with 15 business consultants who had limited or no pricing experience. Let the games begin!

I'm delighted to say, our group experienced enormous success almost from the beginning. By the end of our first year (2005), we had achieved over $300 million in pre-tax profits (which paid for the investment in pricing) — a revenue increase of over 1% from 2004. In subsequent years, we achieved results of roughly $1 billion a year of enhanced profit from pricing actions. In fact, we delivered seven straight years of pricing increases, which included 22 straight quarters of "quarter over quarter" pricing increases followed by only two "down" quarters during the 2009 recession, after which quarterly increases resumed. Our performance is shown in Figure 10. For Six Sigma fans, that represented a statistically significant change in pricing performance. It gave our group, and the company, a reason to feel extremely proud. My first book "The Pricing and Profit Playbook" details this transformation and offers practical advice for other companies seeking superior results from their pricing journey.

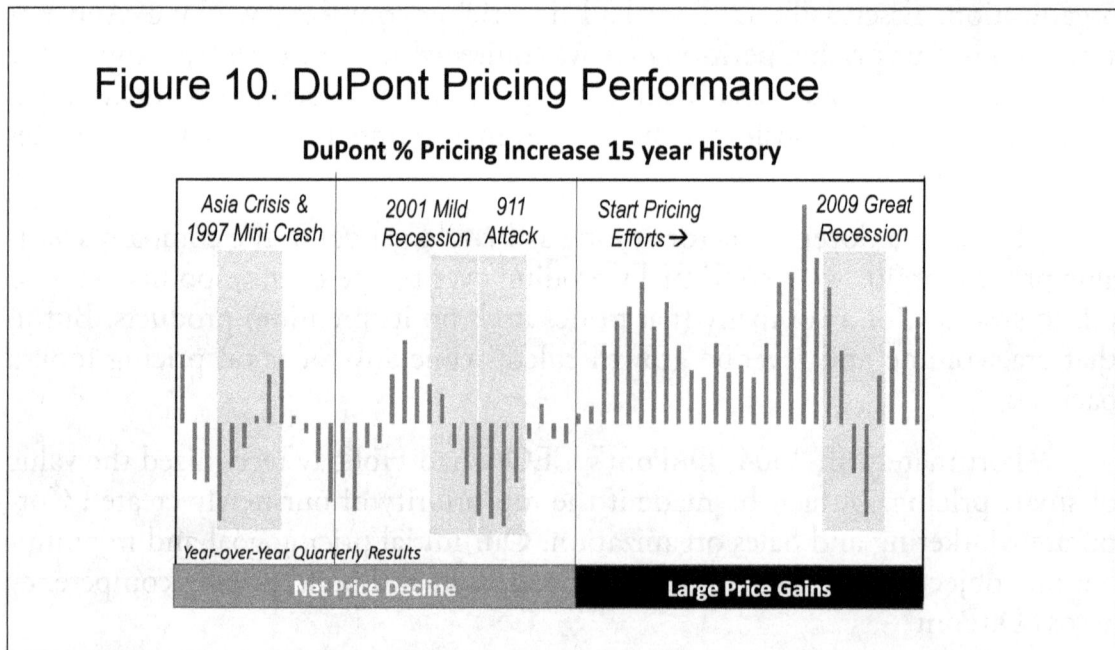

Figure 10. DuPont Pricing Performance

DuPont % Pricing Increase 15 year History

Asia Crisis & 1997 Mini Crash | 2001 Mild Recession | 911 Attack | Start Pricing Efforts → | 2009 Great Recession

Year-over-Year Quarterly Results

Net Price Decline | **Large Price Gains**

Pre-recession, our corporate pricing group aided our businesses by leading price improvement projects business-by-business; we ran deep analysis of their pricing and margin history, examined their market dynamics, and made recommendations to the prices and their policies. We tackled the company culture, leadership behaviors, sales and marketing skills and courage, the lack of embedded pricing resources in businesses, and the improvement of pricing processes and price management systems.

Our businesses shifted from limited price increases with low success rates to frequent (one – four times/year) and highly successful price increases. All based on each business's specific market dynamics and value propositions. It's important to note that during this time, our customer loyalty score (as measured by the Net Promoter Score) actually increased 30%; we were increasing under the best practice guidelines discussed throughout this book that focus on fairness and trust.

Oil prices had been rising at unprecedented rates pre-recession. Downstream derivatives were increasing their prices and most DuPont businesses experienced significant raw material price increases in a few short years. Some experienced over 20% increases. We did pass along these costs to our customers, yet initially we were in a learning curve and thus less effective than we would eventually become. We often took months to implement our increases and even then, didn't always increase sufficiently to off-set our rising costs. Until our pricing skill and courage developed, many large customers successfully negotiated lower price increases then was fair to DuPont. But just before the recession, we were at the top of our game — increasing rapidly and effectively based on fair market dynamics. We didn't just raise price tied to rising raw material costs. Increases also included measures such as establishing a fair value premium for our superior products or services and taking advantage of tight supply/demand situations or other favorable market dynamics like shared industry pain (e.g., low financial health, rising freight costs).

By early 2008, it was becoming clear to me that a market downturn was likely approaching by year-end. Part of my normal operating processes included meeting with our DuPont economist and our head of procurement on a monthly basis to assess new or projected changes in market dynamics. I also periodically held a network meeting with the marketing leaders of each of our strategic business units — this was a sharing and learning forum.

Our businesses serving the construction industry were one of our early warning flags — they typically experience downturns before the bulk of other DuPont business. The early guidance that I and our chief economist provided to our businesses was two-fold: a market downturn is coming by year-end and any price increases you are planning for 2008 should be done in the first half of the year when market conditions still support fair increases. Throughout the year, I increased the frequency of meetings with marketing leaders, procurement, and our economist.

In early November 2008 I organized and led a "Pricing in a Recession" half-day summit in the U.S. The focus, of course, was how to manage pricing in a recession with confidence. Hundreds of business, marketing, and salespeople attended. It was such a success that the then CEO insisted we roll it out to all regions within the next ten days. We did this through a combination of in-person summits and virtual summits. Much of this work became the foundation for my five-step Pricing Crisis Preparedness Plan.

Our corporate marketing and sales group continued to put out guidance, newsletters, on-demand video's and articles to aid our businesses, in addition to our business-by-business consulting projects. Most of our businesses experienced 20 — 40% market demand declines. Customer pressure to reduced price soared. In fact, customers threatened to shift to new suppliers if we didn't drop our prices. So, using newly developed approaches, we selectively dropped our prices, carefully and thoughtfully, to minimize the necessary price decline. We identified pockets of products or markets where we could hold or even increase price. (During this recession, most chemical companies had to drop price to remain competitive.)

By March 2009, we held another half-day summit still focused on pricing in a recession and rolled it out globally. This session had a large component of making trade-off decisions. Different functions of DuPont were all pushing hard on different objectives such as "improve our cash flow, reduce inventory, and shorten payment terms", "increase volume sales to keep our manufacturing plants running at a reasonable unit cost" and "sell more volume to make up for the declining market size." We needed to provide frameworks that allowed us to juggle all these objectives in a way that optimized our company profitability and cash flow.

By later 2009, my subsequent summit focus turned to "pricing in a recovery." Varying businesses and regions were seeing the light at the end of the tunnel, and once again, we proactively wanted to manage our pricing for optimized profits. Pricing in a recovery requires different strategies and tactics. We went back to our five-step preparedness plan and refined it for these changing dynamics. As the economy picked up in late 2009 and early 2010, we carefully brought prices back up to pre-recession pricing and beyond.

Our businesses faced these tough markets with courage. They effectively dealt with very aggressive competitors — those targeting share growth at the expense of Dupont. They continued to proactively communicate to their customer base in an attempt to lower anxiety, set expectations, and build trust. The result was surprising and unprecedented. As mentioned earlier, despite some quarters of lost pricing, we gained $200 million in profits over our 2008 prices.

Comparing this performance to other difficult market times that DuPont historically faced is even more impressive. Figure 10 highlights the mild 2001 recession, the 1997 mini-crash and a few other difficult times — times where we faced significant raw material declines and the resultant customer price pressure that goes along with those situations. Historically, we lost price and large profits each and every time we faced difficult situations. We were slow to recover after the crisis. Yet in the great recession, the most dire of tough times, we gained profit for the year. The five-step plan, along with the sales skills, courage, and confidence made an enormous difference.

It's also interesting to note that during the recession DuPont, after much agonizing, shutdown several of our older, less technically advanced and higher-cost plants permanently. We did not need them with the low market demand in 2009, yet we knew it would be difficult to operate without this capacity when the markets returned to their normal levels. In fact, post the recovery we were not able to meet full demand and had to slightly limit our sales. Yet surprisingly (or not so much to a pricing expert), our total profits were much higher while we were selling less volume! We raised our price with more confidence and as mentioned earlier in this book, price is a much larger lever to effect profits than volume.

When we shifted our mental models away from 'we must sell out our assets, even if that means we need to lower our price to a point that makes that possible' to 'there is no extra product to sell so I can confidently negotiate for the fair value price I deserve,' we found we could do amazing things. And, you can as well if you develop your pricing skills and courage.

You now have the guidance to prepare your Pricing Crisis Preparedness Plan. Hopefully, you have also been inspired and developed the confidence needed to successfully influence your market in a positive direction.

However, if you remain skeptical about your ability to influence the market or uncertain on how to proceed, no worries. This book, as stated initially, is a concise study guide written predominantly for resources with reasonably strong pricing knowledge. And, even if you get it, you may struggle with how to convince the rest of your leadership or sales teams. You, or your company, may benefit from additional reading, training courses, or consulting.

Suggested Reading and Resources

Joanne M. Smith, *The Price Negotiation Playbook,* Bradley Publishing 2018

Price to Profits Consulting (Joanne M. Smith, President): For On-site or Live Online Training & Strategy Workshops or consulting engagements.

Professional Pricing Society: On-site Conference Workshops and web-based training sessions including pricing certifications for pricing, marketing and sales organizations.

About the Author

Smith spent over 20 years driving profitability from a variety of business, marketing, and pricing leadership roles inside of DuPont. As the Corporate Director of Marketing and Pricing at DuPont, she headed a highly innovative pricing team that influenced senior leaders including those in the marketing and sales organizations to adopt new, bold pricing approaches.

Currently, she is president of Price to Profits Consulting, LLC (www.price2profits.com) which assists B2B companies in transforming their pricing performance to enhance long-term profitability. Joanne is the author of *The Price Negotiation Playbook* and *The Price and Profit Playbook*. She consults on pricing strategy, teaches pricing courses, as well as provides keynote speeches, around the world.

Joanne also teaches for the Professional Pricing Society and their certified pricing program as well as the Institute for the Study of Business Markets.

Joanne resides in Avondale, Pennsylvania. She can be reached at joanne-smith@price2profits.com